T0146988

POP'S PIER

POP'S PIER

DONNA CALHOUN

POP'S PIER

iUniverse books may be ordered through booksellers or by contacting:

iUniverse
1663 Liberty Drive
Bloomington, IN 47403
www.iuniverse.com
1-800-Authors (1-800-288-4677)

Because of the dynamic nature of the internet, any web addresses or links contained in this book may have changed since publication and may no longer be valid. The views expressed in this work are solely those of the author and do not necessarily reflect the views of the publisher, and the publisher hereby disclaims any responsibility for them.

The views expressed in this work are solely those of the author and do not necessarily reflect the views of the publisher, and the publisher hereby disclaims any responsibility for them.

Any people depicted in stock imagery provided by Getty Images are models, and such images are being used for illustrative purposes only.
Certain stock imagery © Getty Images.

ISBN: 978-1-5320-7518-6 (sc)
ISBN: 978-1-5320-7519-3 (e)

Library of Congress Control Number: 2019906729

Print information available on the last page.

iUniverse rev. date: 06/14/2019

To my dad, Byron Calhoun

It is more important to love *people* than to love things!

AUTHOR'S NOTE

None of the names have been changed, because there are *no* innocent people to be protected here. However, most of the stories included in this book have been passed down over many years. They have been embellished, exaggerated, inflated, magnified, and overblown, and in some cases, they might be outright lies. I have no way to know because I was just a kid listening to grown-ups tell stories from my bedroom when I should have been asleep.

The purpose of the book is to let you know what an amazing man my dad was and to celebrate all the friendships and love he gave us ... and you gave him.

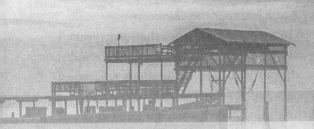

POP'S PIER

I've been standing on this long wooden pier for a lifetime. I know that must sound like an overstatement, but it is true. I've overlooked the muddy brown water of Mobile Bay for seven decades.

Today there is a slight breeze, but nobody is on the water yet. It is still early in the morning, and the boats will start coming soon. They always do this time of year. It's only the second of June, but summer in Alabama is here.

When I first started fishing these waters as kid, there wasn't the number of people there are now. It's sad that we have lost that peace and quiet, but it is good that the young people like Gracie, Korra, and Fallon now love the water as much as I did when I was their age. But I'm getting ahead of myself.

I have seen it all over the years from the end of this pier—sailboats, tugboats, Jet Skis, yachts. I've seen every type of boat that you can imagine and every type of captain sporting them. I've watched the captains who work boats like they are extensions of their own bodies, captains who can read the water and the wind like surgeons read x-rays, looking for the answers in the lines of the currents and the flow of the clouds just as surgeons look for the lines of bones and the flow of the blood. Unfortunately, I have also seen the captains who run aground in these shallow bay waters or hit piers trying to navigate at night without proper training. Some of these captains are my friends. I've helped them when they have pulled up to the end of my pier. I've watched as the coast guard chased them down and then towed them in. My wife and I have spent hours on this pier trying to figure out the stories of the people we have watched over the years.

This is my pier. It has been in my family for more than fifty years. I have built it back probably twenty times during those years. The wooden pier has grown bigger with each reconstruction. It has been redesigned many times for different purposes, but the one constant about this pier is that it has always made me and mine happy when we walked, sat, or lay on it in the sunlight or moonlight. My pier shares its vigil with other piers on Mobile Bay. I know every pier to the east and to the west of us as far as the eye can see. The owners of these piers have changed, and the piers themselves have seen more interesting sights than most two-by-fours throughout the world.

These piers and their owners don't last very long here in Alabama. Hurricanes chase about 25 percent of them away, and the high price of waterfront property chases the other percentage away. The only folks who can afford to buy here are the investors. The landscape has changed; condos are everywhere. The people have changed. Yankees are everywhere. The attitude has changed. Drunken ex-patriots who fancy themselves as present-day pirates are everywhere. But I am still here. I am here with my family, my friends, and my love of the water.

I have stayed through the last fifty years. A lot has changed for me in those years. I've lost my son who grew up here. Most of my friends have either left or died. The one constant companion through the years has been the love of my life, a woman who sixty years ago became my bride and is still my girlfriend today. My wife and my pier, those have been the two stable factors in my life for more than half a century. They both have changed a great deal. Both have shifted in places that were once straight. They both dip a little in the middle. They are both a little scarred and weathered, but it just adds character to them both.

Standing on this old pier is a good way for me to reflect. And I've got the time to do just that today. I have some things that I need to say, and this is just the right place for this discussion. Sit back. Put up your feet, and open a cold beer if you've got one. I have some things to share before I move off this hundred-foot stretch of wood.

I need to tell a story, and hopefully, you will find it interesting.

CHAPTER 1

From where I stand on this pier, I can look across Mobile Bay and see the point south of Fairhope, Alabama. On a good night, you can see the lights of the Grand Hotel in Point Clear, which brings back the memories of Civil War sailors and Captain Farragut yelling, "Damn the torpedoes. Full speed ahead," during the battle of Mobile Bay.

I've been standing here and looking out into the water for a while now. I've lost track of time, so I'm not sure how long I've been out here. The sun was just coming up when I got here, and though I don't remember the trip here, it is a fact that this place makes me happy, and oftentimes when I've come here over the years, I couldn't remember the traffic or the tourist who got in the way.

The challenge to get here is always erased by the peace and joy of my arrival at this destination. I don't remember sitting in line at the fifty stoplights between this pier or my beach house and my permanent home, which is up the road a piece. It is worth the long trip just to be able to stand here and look out at the water. This place is calming and serene. I've lived on the water all my life, and I truly believe that once you have lived on a body of water, whether it is a bay or a river, you must always live on water to be happy. I've heard we are called water babies—those people like me who crave the water and sand like some people crave alcohol. I think that the sound of the surf and the way the sun rising over the water somehow sets into your soul and becomes a part of you. Once you are truly possessed by the water, you will never be complete if you are unfortunate enough to find yourself landlocked far from the shore.

We purchased this property in the early 1960s, and back then when we first started coming here, it was a major adventure just to get on this island. It was not the popular tourist attraction that it is today. This island is called Pleasure Island by the Chamber of Commerce. It is better known as Gulf Shores or Fort Morgan, Alabama, to anyone who has ever visited or read a *Southern Living* magazine.

One of the great things about being a destination for tourist dollars is that the state of Alabama has put a great deal of money into making the trip onto the island a lot easier. To get on the island back in the 1960s, you had to take a bridge across the Intracoastal Waterway that ran between the island and the mainland of Foley. It was not really a drawbridge that lifted into the air but a bridge that would pivot from right to left, leaving the bridge parallel to the middle of the Intracoastal Waterway. The bridge then became an island itself, and the only resident of the island was the gatekeeper in the bridge house. The passageway of either side allowed tugboats with their massive barges and sailboats with their high masts to pass from Mississippi through Mobile Bay and all the way to Florida without having to get into the tumultuous Gulf of Mexico. It's a protected passageway that allows all those boat captains some peace of mind that traveling the unpredictable gulf waters doesn't.

The trip to the island and across the bridge seemed endless on Friday afternoons when the bridge was closed to automobiles for the boat traffic. It was not unusual to spend an hour waiting for tugboats to push barges carrying everything from coal to cargo containers down the waterway. It was maddening for me back then. I was always in a hurry to get to the beach after a long workweek. But my kids always loved that part of the trip, sitting on the hood of the car while we waited and watched the large vessels roll along in no great hurry. The kids were small then, and these boats seemed to be world adventurers to them. Hell, now my daughter works for a company out of Hong Kong and travels Asia and the South Pacific regularly. It's hard to believe that same kid would sit and wave at every boat like they were the most amazing things and now she lives in a place where she is the foreigner.

The kids would wave, and the boat captains would wave back. The kids in all the cars in line would get out and run to the edge of the water, yelling and calling frantically until the tugboat captains blew their massive foghorns. There would be a line of cars waiting on both sides of the swinging bridge, but most people didn't mind too much back then. Life was slower, and getting in a rush just wasn't part of the plan. Now the tourist will run you over going eighty miles an hour down Highway 59, hurrying to the beach on Friday afternoon so they can be the first ones to get there to relax. Now it's nice to be my age and not in a hurry about much of anything.

When we first started coming to Gulf Shores with my beautiful wife and two toddler children in the early '60s, it took a good two hours or more to get from our place in Fairhope on the eastern shore of Mobile Bay to the island and then down Fort Morgan Road to our piece of sand. We drove east from Fairhope and then south to Gulf Shores and then west again down Fort Morgan Road. Two hours later we ended up due south of where we'd started, but as they say, you can't get here from there. You have to go somewhere else to start.

When you stand on the end of this pier and look north, you are looking at Point Clear, Alabama, just south of Fairhope. If you're not from around here, you may not know how beautiful our little Mobile Bay was in those days. Any newcomers would assume that the water has always been this shade of brown, but it wasn't. In the '60s, you could see the fish swimming under this pier and the crabs inching their way from one post to the next in search of something to eat. The water was clear and blue. The oysters and fish were plentiful.

I remember when my wife and her mother, Merle, came up with the crazy idea to buy a piece of property on the desolate little finger of land called Fort Morgan Road. My father-in-law had made the very valid point that this was Baldwin County, and as "anyone with any amount of brain in their pretty little heads knows, sand was good for absolutely nothing. You can't grow potatoes or watermelons in sand." My father-in-law's family had been farmers in Baldwin County for generations, and sand was worthless to them. But believe me—you don't know what stubborn is until you have met a southern belle in general and in particular a female Neumann, my wife's maiden name. These two ladies knew that they wanted a place at the beach, and they were going to have it regardless of what my father-in-law or I had to say about it. They were stubborn southern women, and we men would be better off to just keep our mouths shut.

My father-in-law, Eric Neumann, had grown up in Baldwin County in a little community north and east of Gulf Shores called Elberta. That part of the county was like the rest of Baldwin County at that time—farmland. It was rich, productive, moneymaking potato farmland.

Eric and his brothers had all come over from Germany on a slow boat under the terrible conditions of sickness and poverty and into Ellis Island's New York harbor in 1909. The boat was an old wooden cargo carrier that was converted to carry people. They said that people were treated more like animals on that passage than like humans. The boats were overcrowded and without quality food or water. When passengers were sick, there was no seasick mediation that they could take and not enough room to lie down for rest. Even into his eighties, Eric remembered the trip. He has passed on now, and if I was talking to anyone other than my wife, I'd say that I missed the old guy. However, I'd never admit to her that I missed her father.

In his later years, he turned into a bit of a guru and had all the answers for everything, which drove me crazy. I was a professional businessman, and he had always worked for himself. I didn't understand the wisdom of his years just like my kids didn't appreciate the wisdom I'd tried to give them over the years. But now that I've had some time to think about it all, I've got to admit that I kind of miss the guy.

Eric was only seven years old on that trip from Germany to America. At the time, he and his brothers didn't speak a word of English when they arrived in New York. The conditions on land at the time under the watchful eye of the Stature of Liberty were not much better than on the boat. Eric told stories of being herded into a warehouse that was larger than a barn to be examined like livestock and sprayed for lice and appraised like animals to pass into the country. They had no money to speak of, so they had traveled as inexpensively as possible on the boat. They didn't have the fin stabilizer like they do on the cruise ships today. You felt every roll of the ship, so seasickness was the norm. When you added food that was marginal and being scared to the rolling stomachs, it was torture in good weather and worse than imaginable in bad.

Eric's mother and father, along with seven boys, were met at the docks by his uncle, who had come to the States several years earlier. Other members of the family had come across to the United States over the eighteen months before Eric's family and had settled in Alabama with a large German community. When they met their uncle in New York, the kids climbed into a truck and rode in the back of that pickup for a week to reach south Alabama.

They had done all of this to escape prewar Germany for a better life—the better life that they had come to included farming potatoes for sixteen hours a day without the benefit of modern equipment or the advantages of hired help. Thank goodness his father had seven boys. Girls were of little value to a farm family in those days. The boys gave the farm lots of hands but very little experienced help. Eric was seven and had two younger brothers. Everyone worked. Unlike today, there were no video games or cell phones, so working the farm was pretty much all there was to do.

The boys learned farming quickly, but Eric knew he was not cut out to be a lifelong farmer. He worked well with his hands and discovered early that he had a knack for building furniture. He also used those hands to become a banjo player at a local pub. During the day for six days a week, the boys all worked the farm, but on Saturday nights, Eric would play banjo at the pub. The pub was really just an old farmhouse with wooden floors and a sagging front porch that somebody had turned into a pub. Nobody really worried that he was too young to be in a bar. It was the depression, and Eric was making more in tips than most people made in their regular salary. Then on Sunday morning the whole family would attend the local Baptist church and spend most of the day with their church family.

As you can imagine, when my wife and her mother had suggested that we put $3,000 down on one acre of land on an island where there were no crops and the soil was worthless for farming, my father-in-law thought that they had lost their minds. The arguments that ensued between the lot of them were heated. But the women were persistent, refusing to take no for an answer. They had come up with $2,000 out of pin money and had borrowed the other thousand on a short-term loan.

Forty years later my father-in-law is no longer here for my wife to say, "I told you so," but if he were here, I would happily stand by while she had the pleasure of telling him that the supposedly worthless land is now worth more a foot than the total they paid for their farm property. It is worth more a foot than an acre of his rich farm. I wonder what the crazy German would say about that.

Standing here on this pier, I must admit that a great deal of work and worry has gone into the fifty years of owning this place, but the memories and pleasure of it all is what I'm here to talk about today. It is mind-numbing to think of all the enjoyment and celebration that has happened here on this worthless land. The friends who have come and gone during those years are too numerous to count. The parties were mostly too racy to tell you about, but we'll get to them anyway. I'm old now, seventy-nine years old, and old men have no secrets.

One of my best friends during the first thirty years of having this place was my next-door neighbor, a worldly and wise gentleman named Obie Rush. Obie bought his acres of land the year before my wife and her mother bought our land. Over the years Obie and my wife had continued to purchase the whole damn neighborhood, one more acre at a time. We accumulated ten acres before we decided that enough was enough and stopped buying out the neighbors. The Rushes did not. My wife's motivation was a sound investment, which it obviously has been, but Obie's motivation was buying it all to keep people he didn't like off his island. And there were a lot of people Obie didn't like. In fact, there were very few people he admitted that he did like.

Obie was a good ten years older than me and had lived on the bay all his life as I had. He was a crusty old southern codger who reminded me of Hemingway's *Old Man and the Sea*. Obie had been gray headed since the day I met him, with a jolly beer belly that he worked hard to earn and keep. Obie was a conservative Republican in the Deep South when people who voted that way were too embarrassed to admit it in public. He walked with the slow, sure steps of a man who knew where he was going but wasn't in a big hurry to get there. He talked in a low, calm voice that made you stop and listen regardless of the subject. And talking on the pier was one of his favorite ways to pass the time. He had been a mentor to me since the first time I shook his hand over a burning pile of sticks and leaves when we were still clearing the lot to build the beach house that stands on the property today.

Between the two of us, we had a good working knowledge of fishing, weather patterns, and the art of mixing a good stiff drink. We could talk for hours sitting on the end of the pier. The favorite topic was our personal philosophy on life, and the colder the beer and the stronger the drinks, the more philosophical we got. Obie and I had gotten in our share of trouble when we were younger, but both of our wives were long past caring about the simple things like us being there on time when we saw the fifth anniversary of being neighbors. We had both mellowed during those years at the beach. We were more like rotten fruit than fine wine.

One day in 1993, Obie had seen me out on the pier on a Friday afternoon. This was not an unusual event as I was on this pier most Friday afternoons during the spring and summer. I was still working then, and my time at the beach house was limited to weekends and vacation time. Obie, who had retired several years before, would normally come over to the pier on Fridays once he saw me get settled with a beer in my hand, and that day in the early '90s was no different.

My normal process of opening the beach house on Friday was to get to the beach, open all the doors and windows, and then check the house for any animals or birds that had taken up residence during the week. The first thing I did for myself was take a case of Miller Lite and a ten-pound bag of ice out to the end of the pier to put in the ice chest that stayed there permanently. Once the beer was iced, I would sit for a minute and let the week roll off me like Alabama red clay rolls off your car in a hard rainstorm.

It was holding the cold beer in my hand and looking over the water that let me know it was truly the weekend. Years ago I had purchased *Dad's ice chest* for the end of the pier, which held my treasure chest of adult beverages. Everyone called it that. Even people who didn't call me Dad called the ice chest on the end of the pier Dad's ice chest. And everyone seemed to know that the first thing you did when you came to the beach was fill it up with Miller Lite or whatever brand you might like. Putting the beer in the cooler was symbolic of arriving for the weekend. It was the most important symbol of putting the workweek behind you and immersing yourself in the full experience of a weekend at the beach, which everyone knows is better than a weekend anywhere else.

It was funny watching people who had come to the beach a couple of times. They understood that Dad's ice chest was not a place for Cokes or bottled water. It is a beer cooler. It has always been full and always cold. We have purchased a number of Dad's ice chests over the fifty years that we have been sitting on this pier, but they always had the same qualities. They are round, they have tight lids on them, and they always sit in the same place on the end of the pier, specifically under the small table on a center post that held up a partial roof. Dad's ice chest has always been the focal point of the communal area on the end of this pier. It is the center of attention, and it is as important to the beach experience as the water and the sand.

If you open the ice chest right now, you'll find nice cold beer, and you'll know all is right with the world. It makes me smile just thinking about it. I don't remember putting the beer in the cooler this time, but I have trained many a minion over the years, mostly my daughters' boyfriends, on the process, and it's possible that it was one of them that remembered to add the beer and ice for me this time.

Let's get back to the story of Obie in '93. He had joined me that day, and he was more serious than normal. I figured that he had read something disturbing in the newspaper or seen something on the news that upset him. Obie was a man of questionable politics, but he was principled and thoughtful just the same. He would regularly get upset about the most minor things that happened in our community. He loved this country and this island. He had grown up as I had on Mobile Bay and knew that the changes he was seeing were not going to have positive long-term effects on the area.

Obie was an environmentalist before anyone in Hollywood found out that it was fashionable and started using salad dressing as a platform for environmental concerns. He was possibly the first tree hugger I knew. Greenpeace had nothing on this man. It was this passion that made him run for the office of county building inspector. He had become very concerned about the amount of building that had occurred on Pleasure Island after Hurricane Frederick in the fall of 1979. Our quite little island, which was the best kept secret in Alabama for many years, changed completely after that storm. It seemed for a long time nobody in the rest of the country knew that Alabama had sugary white beaches just like Florida. When we got national attention during the hurricane coverage, it seemed that the rest of the world discovered we were here. Hurricane Frederick changed everything, and suddenly, a new form of vagabond or carpetbagger descended on our secret southern beaches—the developer. They came in with the same lack of grace and dignity that Sherman used when he burned his way through Atlanta, destroying everything in his path.

They had destroyed the small fishing villages of Gulf Shores and Orange Beach, building condominiums everywhere that they could pilfer a deed from a family, using a suitcase full of Ben Franklins as incentive to make grandmas give up the deeds to the properties that had been in their families for years. Whole families of otherwise loving people broke up over the fight for these plots of sand that nobody wanted only a couple of years before. The peaceful little Redneck Rivera had become the new Miami Beach, and Obie didn't like it one bit.

Obie would wax philosophically for hours on the end of this pier and talk about the horror of it all. Well, he would continue as long as there was cold beer in Dad's ice chest. Once that ran out, he generally went home to his wife, Gloria, who really didn't want to hear it. On this day I remember Obie coming over with a solemn look, which was not normal for him. This look was not angry or grumpy over politics. This was an unusual look and concerned me greatly. Obie was generally a happy yet opinionated guy who was more concerned about local fishing regulations than world events. I asked him to take a seat, and we talked of unimportant things. I offered him a cold beer while I waited to see what was on his mind.

"Byron," he said, looking at the slats on the deck of the wood pier as if he had never seen two-by-fours before. "I'm sick."

This did not come as a great surprise to me. I had noticed that he had been having a lot of doctor's appointments that seemed to take him off the island to Mobile regularly. Local doctors at this time could take care of most medical issues, but when anyone said that they were going to the doctor in Mobile, it was going to be something more than just your average summer flu or broken bone. Gulf Shores did not have a full-time physician. You had to go up the road a piece to Foley to get to a real doctor. A lot of the good physicians had bought houses at the beach, and many were opening offices on the island so that they could justify the weekends at the beach; however, that was a couple of years in the future.

"I figure I've got about a year to live." Obie was known to have a flair for drama, and I figured one year probably meant ten. So I listened and didn't say anything.

"I have a favor to ask you, my friend. And nobody—and I mean nobody—can be trusted with this favor other than you." Obie paused for great dramatic effect and took a long drink of his beer. Actually, it was my beer, but who was counting?

"You must promise me that you will grant this, my dying wish." From the sound of it, he was seeing the white lights and tunnel right then, so I thought it a good idea to agree immediately.

"Sure, Obie. Anything, my friend. Just tell me, and I'll do it." I made sure that my tone had a grievous note to it for good measure. Even the boy who cried wolf eventfully got eaten by one. I didn't mean to minimize his condition as it turned out he was ill and making plans was a good idea, though I didn't believe it at the time.

"I have a plan. You know, for when I'm gone." He stopped and took another draw from his beer. "I've written it all into my will, and I've given it to Gloria." I could just imagine Gloria, his wife, rolling her eyes at this unfolding Shakespearean tragedy.

"When I'm gone I need you to get my tombstone and place it out by the road." The road he was talking about was Fort Morgan Road. It was a twenty-two-mile peninsula that ends at Fort Morgan, an actual Confederate Civil War fort. It was a single-lane road then, and most of it still is today.

"I'm going to order my tombstone tomorrow, and it will be paid for. The guy in Foley will have all my last wishes on what to engrave on the tombstone." All of this seemed like a bit much, but I continued to listen.

"Then I need you to promise that you will spread my ashes over Mobile Bay, right off the end of my pier. This is where I have been the happiest and where I want to be. Throw me right into the bay." He told me with a sweeping motion over the water to make sure I understood how to spread his ashes.

"No problem, Obie. I got it brother. You can count on me." Then thinking about what he was suggesting, putting his tombstone on a busy two-lane road like Fort Morgan Road, I asked, "By the way, what is your tombstone going to say?"

"Come on down," he said.

And so it did. To this day, if you come down Fort Morgan Road to the ten-mile marker, you will see a tombstone on the right-hand side of the drive that says, "Come on down."

It was seven years after that discussion on the end of my pier that Obie passed. He really wasn't as sick as he thought, and when he died, Gloria and I did exactly as he wished. One beautiful, clear day, we spread his ashes on the rippling waves of Mobile Bay as the tide rolled out of the bay, taking Obie Rush out to the Gulf of Mexico.

Obie is but one of my friends who deserves to have his story told. There are many more, and we'll get to them too.

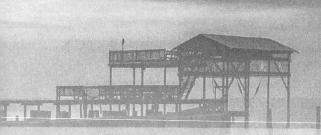

CHAPTER 2

It was August 8, 1967, when we finally cleared a path from Fort Morgan Road to our beach on Mobile Bay for the first time. I remember this day because we had worked for a full summer to clear away brush and trees on the lot after we purchased it that spring. We dug up stumps and cacti, fighting and killing snakes to get a single-car driveway all the way from the road to the bay. The whole clearing process had been hot and dusty because all Alabama was like that during the summer months. It gets so hot and humid that working outside and doing hard manual labor was torture. It was that clear, sweltering, hot summer day that we had finished the three-hundred-foot drive-through that allowed us to move the modest mobile home into its resting place overlooking the bay.

The mobile home—we called them trailers back then without being embarrassed about it—was a gift from the American Red Cross. It was a one-bedroom that was a donated hurricane trailer used to collect blood donations and conduct training programs for the nurses that were known as the Red Cross vampires. My mother-in-law had worked for the Red Cross as a bookkeeper, and they had purchased a better model and needed to have the old one hauled off. We agreed to take it off their hands and moved it to the beach. They didn't charge us anything as they just wanted it gone. It was eight feet wide and thirty-five feet long. It looked more like a missile than a mobile home. It was long and silver with only a few small windows. The majority of this house was one long room that included the living room and the kitchen space. There was no walls between these two rooms, so if you were cooking crabs in a spicy crab boil, everybody but the cook had to leave and go outside because it would burn your eyes if you stayed inside.

The camp, as we called it back then, was a one-bedroom, one-bath cramped space for two families. The kitchen was so small my wife called it a "one-butt kitchen" because you couldn't have two people in there at once without bumping into each other. It was all we needed at the time because we cooked most meals outside on the grill. During the summer months, it was impossible to breathe inside when the pots were boiling, and the smell of fried fish filled the confided space. Even with all the small windows open, the spices would make your eyes water. The kitchen only had three feet of counter space and a mobile home refrigerator.

We only had a small refrigerator, which made ice chests vital for a weekend at the beach. The ice chest became the most valuable thing in the car each trip, last thing to go into the car leaving Fairhope and the first thing to come out of the car when we got to the beach. In those days of being ten miles away from the closest store, you couldn't just run down the block to get anything you needed. If you didn't bring it, you didn't need it. It was a planned trip to make the ten-mile trip into Gulf Shores from the beach house.

Because we only had one bedroom inside the trailer and that was used by my in-laws, we quickly decided that a sleeping porch was necessary. We built a sleeping porch that was ten feet wide and ran the entire length of the trailer. With this one addition of a cement floor, wooden walls, and a lot of screen, which was the only ventilation, we more than doubled our living space in the first six months. At each end of the porch, we placed bunk beds that we'd purchased from the navy base in Pensacola for ten dollars each. They had once been occupied by sailors and now held our precious children. The kids thought the bunk beds were very cool and climbed like monkeys from one level to the other.

For the middle of the porch, we purchased two foldout sofa beds that could be folded up during the day and let out for sleeping at night. The rule was that the sofa beds stayed folded until after everyone had their showers at night to save on the limited space. Once the sofa beds were folded out, you really could move very well from one end of the porch to the other.

We only had one shower, and it was big enough for a small child to turn around in; however, large adults would need to wash half their bodies at a time. We also had a large metal washtub outside for when the kids were small, but they quickly outgrew that setup. If someone forgot the rule about unfolding the beds and let them out early, it became an obstacle course to get from one end of the porch to the other. You had to climb over sofa beds to get to the bunk beds on the opposite end of the porch. Being at the beach, sand was always a problem. So once you were comfortable in bed, anyone with sandy feet crawling across your bed would cause a major battle regardless of whether it was intentional or not. The sleeping porch was the first addition to the mobile home but not the last.

Once we had the camp in order with the new addition, the yard became my passion. As I said, it had taken many months to cut through the tropical brush to get a clear path to the beach. Once the camp was set up, I started working on the yard. We always refer to the front yard for any beach property as the beach side. When you entered the property from the road, you were actually in the backyard. This would cause great confusion among our guests who referred to the way you entered the house as the front yard.

The front yard was my annual battlefield. At first, we had to get to the beach by walking through the narrow grass path, which was a minefield of sandspurs and wild cacti that would reach out and grab you, taking you immediately to a sitting position until you could get the microscopic stickers out of your feet. Numerous guests would each ask, "How can anything so small cause so much pain?" It took me years to get the yard under control and remove all the cacti that came back every year for twenty years. We finally were able to plant grass and clear away enough to see the beautiful mossy cedar trees that Alabama is famous for. There is no way to describe the view from the house, looking through the mossy trees to the clear blue water of Mobile Bay. It was heaven to us.

We were not rich people. The fact that we had a home in the city and a place at the beach seemed silly to most people back then, but to us and my in-laws, it was always meant to be a fishing camp, nothing more. My wife and her mother bought it as a place to raise their children and grandchildren like we were all raised—on the water, respecting the marine life and enjoying the fun that it provided. I learned to fish on Mobile Bay, and my kids learned to fish on Mobile Bay. The water fed my family and friends many weekends during the summer. This water provided me with my first job and will hopefully be the last thing I see before I close my eyes permanently.

Now so many years have passed by. My son has been gone for more than thirty years from a motorcycle accident, and my daughter lives halfway around the world for her job. The maintenance of this place has fallen to me and my wife. It is a major project just to stay ahead of the grass that I once fought so hard to get started. I'm proud of who and what my kids have become, but I miss the old days of being the guy with all the answers—teaching my son to fish with a small rod, watching the kids as they lie facedown on the pier and stare over the edge for crabs walking underneath, throwing the cast net with my son for hours in the shallow water and then cooking mullet on the grill for everyone.

My daughter had cross-stitched a saying for me when she was eighteen years old that still hangs on the wall in the camp's living room today. It was for some birthday, or maybe it was for Father's Day. Who remembers those kinds of things this many years later? It said,

Age Six "My daddy knows everything."
Age Thirteen "My daddy is so old fashion! what does he know?"
Age Nineteen "Dad doesn't have a clue."
Age Twenty-Six "Maybe Dad knows a few things."
Age Thirty-Six "I need to get Dad's opinion on this."
Age Forty-Six "I decided not to make a decision until I speak with Dad."

This had pretty much defined my relationship with my daughter, even though she didn't know how true it would become when she first stitched those words. I think she knows now. I have become the guy with the answers again—that is, until I got sick.

As I sit here on this pier, looking at the mullet jumping under my feet in the water, I'm smiling at the thought that the road has been long but the journey has been fun. Like the front yard of the house, my life has been a constant project to grow and cultivate, making something nice out of something that was a hard struggle, prickly and dangerous in places but worth the beautiful view in the end.

Like our yard, we cultivated and grew the friendships of our neighbors at the beach as well. To our left was the Rushes, Obie and Gloria with their little girl Kathy, and to our right was the Swamp Lady.

As I've said, we purchased the one-acre lot that the house sits on in 1967. Twenty years later my wife was looking at the property tax records for Baldwin County listed in the newspaper. At that time in our county when landowners didn't pay their property taxes, the county posted to the public the names, property locations, and amounts that were due. This was to give the landowners reasonable notice that they owe money before the property was taken by the county and sold for taxes. My wife noticed that the land next to ours had not paid their taxes for many years, and she contacted an attorney about buying the land. This property was roughly nine acres of undeveloped swampland, but it had 750 feet of sand on the water. We paid the back property taxes owed and continued to pay property taxes on the land for another several years before we were able to get a quit claim deed, and eventually, we owned it. This purchase gave us a total of ten acres of land with 850 feet of waterfront beach property. My wife has always been the smart one, and she had managed to purchase nine acres for the cost of the property taxes with patience.

The swamp, as we called it, was a natural habitat for many different birds and animals, including raccoons, alligators, and Canada geese. It was heaven for bullfrogs, and at night they would get so loud that newcomers to the beach would complain that they couldn't sleep with the racket the frogs made while they tossed and turned in their beds.

A couple of years ago, my wife and I were sitting on the pier one morning around nine o'clock, and a marine biologist named Guilford drove up in his Alabama Conservation Association green Ford pickup. He got out of the truck and walked over to the pier where we sat. We invited him to sit down and talk for a minute, and he asked if we would mind if he took a walk through the swampland. We told him that the thing was full of snakes and God only knew what else, but he said he wanted to look anyway. He was as excited as a puppy that needed to pee as he got into his waders and thigh-high boots. We watched as he went in. We sat there, waiting for him to come back out, but it was well after noontime when he splashed back out of that brown swamp water and onto the sandy beach.

Mr. Guilford was ecstatic. He said it was the healthiest swamp he had seen in a long time. We just shook our heads and smiled. We had no idea whether that was a good thing or a bad thing. Over the years we have had several environmentalists survey that piece of wetlands. It seems to draw a lot of interest from developers as well. But we have held on because it blocks us from everyone else.

The other thing we got when we purchased the swamp property was another neighbor—the Swamp Lady. About the time that we were signing that quit claim deed on the swamp, a lady named Nancy bought the hundred feet on the other side of the newly acquired property next to ours. Because the way to get to Nancy's house was down the beach that bordered the swamp, she became known as the Swamp Lady. She was a beautiful city girl from Louisiana who quickly became a member of our beach family. Nancy was about our age and a good listener. We would sit for hours with her and eventually, her guy Doug, talking about all the things they had done and the places we had been. They were an easy couple to like, and we have been friends for many years because of this little piece of heaven. My wife and Nancy were both politicians and liked to share stories about the drama of government life and horrible campaigns.

The one thing about owning a place at the beach is that you are either fixing what is broken or trying to stay ahead of what might break next. The Swamp Lady was a southern belle who had never fixed a busted pipe in her life and had no idea where to start. She could throw a party that would impress a queen, but she had no idea about turning wrenches. I became her Mr. Fix-It in Alabama. Even years later when she was married to a city man named Doug, I would get a phone call on Saturday morning with an odd opening question like "How do we locate our septic tank?" It was a five-minute walk down the beach, and a cup of coffee was the only charge for my consulting services. Over the years Doug borrowed tools, asked a thousand questions, and gave me more laughs than I could count.

Doug was notorious for sinking anything that could float. He sunk boats, Jet Skis, powerboats, and kayaks. Anything that should be on the top of the water, Doug made into a submarine. It was fun to watch what he would buy next, and we would joke about how long it would last. He is an amazingly brilliant businessman who had a gift for making you look forward to seeing him whenever you got the chance. He tells stories that make me say, "No shit?" over and over again.

The most fun that we had with the Swamp Lady and Doug was hunting for buried treasures. One year on the Fourth of July weekend, Nancy and Doug were bringing friends of theirs to the beach—a young couple with two small children. Doug and Jackie made up the story for the children that his ancestors were pirates and that the pirates used their property on Fort Morgan to hide their treasures. Doug called us one night about a week before the Fourth of July weekend and asked if I could bury some *treasure* on the vacant beach between our two houses. We were so excited. My wife found an old box and loaded it with trinkets like plastic bracelets, a plastic pirate sword, and fake gold coins from Mardi Gras for the children to find.

The kids got to the beach late on Friday night and barely slept a wink. The next morning they were up at first light to search for the treasure that they were sure that the pirates had left many years before. It only took one treasure hunt, and a tradition was born. We had done this for several years for many different kids. Doug would call me on a Monday or Tuesday, and I would go bury the *treasure* on Friday afternoon before they got to the beach that night. We would always put a big X in the sand to mark the spot just like the treasure maps. The kids would arrive buzzing with energy to find the treasure. The next day they would all search for the treasure and find it in the sand on the beach. Each year we moved the spot.

This went on for several years before I figured out another way to entertain myself with Doug. He began to bury his own treasure after a couple of years when the kids got older, and Doug and Nancy were able to come over a day before the kids arrived. I was sitting on the pier and watching Doug bury the treasure one day, and I thought, *Wouldn't it be a great idea if after Doug was done I moved the treasure!* And I did.

The next morning the kids and Doug dug in three different spots before they found the treasure, but we all got a good laugh watching him lose his mind for those forty-five minutes it took to find the right spot.

CHAPTER 3

A face appeared in the small window beside the door of the hospital room.

"Sorry to bother you, but I wanted to let you know that the doctor will be here shortly. He is making his rounds down the hall," said the second-floor nurse from Thomas Hospital in Fairhope.

The nurse was a young woman of twenty-five, but like all nurses, she was growing old fast from the exposure to death and illness. She wore a colorful flower-print top with pale blue scrub pants. The woman who had been sitting in the room wondered when nurses stopped wearing those white uniforms. The nurse did wear the white tennis shoes that made those squeaking noises when she walked. That was how the lady in the chair knew that the nurse was coming before she saw her face in the little window.

"Thank you, Jennifer," answered the woman as she put her bookmark back into the copy of the latest Patterson novel.

She looked over at the shape in the bed beside her. He was smaller and frailer than what seemed possible. She reached for the pasty white hand, thinking it was usually so tanned by this time of year.

"The doctor is on his way," she said, giving the hand a pat. "I love you, baby," she said, but she didn't know if she was heard or not.

Jennifer turned and walked out of the room. She had read the charts and seen the results of the test. She knew the news that the doctor was bringing was not good. She felt for this woman; however, there was nothing that she could do, and she knew that it was not her place to tell what she knew. Those conversations are saved for the doctors.

She had listened to hundreds of these discussions and watched the families fall apart. She had been a nurse for a long time, but she had never been able to distance herself from her patients. In nursing school, they said that she would grow hard to the pain and suffering, but she hadn't. Jennifer knew that if she ever got to the point where she didn't care about her patients and their families, she needed to get out of the nursing business and go to work selling real estate.

As she walked out of the room, she saw the doctor down the hall. Just three more rooms to go before this one. She had time to run and make one more call to the woman's daughter and see if she could reach her before the doctor got there.

Back inside the room, the woman sat back comfortably. She had spent a lot of time on this floor of the hospital over the past year. The time she spent here gave her a lot of time to think and remember. She had made all the phone calls to family and friends. Everybody was on hold. Her only child, her daughter, was on her way. The woman hoped that she would not get here before the doctor was done and had left. Her daughter did not handle these situations well, and she really couldn't handle holding herself together while her daughter fell apart. She prayed for a little traffic to slow down her daughter's progress until she could get herself together.

The woman looked down at her wedding ring. Sixty years they had been married. They didn't have much of a wedding or a honeymoon, but the fifty-year wedding anniversary had made up for it all. She and her daughter had planned every detail. She had finally gotten the wedding cake that she had always wanted. They had it at the Fairhope Art Gallery, which was beautiful, and she had talked her husband into wearing a suit and tie. He was so handsome that day.

The food had been amazing. Everything was catered by the best service in Fairhope. She remembered dancing with the old coot and thinking that she had made the right decision. In the early years of their marriage, she had not been so sure. They were so very poor when they first got married. Their dinner the night of the wedding was hot dogs! They were young and laughed about the hot dogs, but they had never forgotten it and had never assumed that they would not have to go back to hot dogs again.

They had wondered separately and together if they had made a big mistake more than once over the sixty years, but not recently. They didn't even doubt their decision when he was so sick, and it took everything she could do to take care of him. There were times recently when he was so unsteady on his feet that she had to walk him from room to room. His health had taken a toll on her health, but she kept pushing forward. "Just one more day," she prayed. "Give us one more day."

On their first anniversary, they started a tradition. They would have dinner and make a toast. The toast had been the same for sixty years. In the good times and in the hard times, they always used the exact same toast. In the early years, the toast was with Coke. Once they got a little money, it became a toast with wine. For the last twenty years, it had always been champagne, the best they could get. That first year they promised each other with the toast "One more year." It was their way of saying everything. "Things will be better next year." "We can make it through one more year." "These kids will be better behaved next year." "We only have one more year of college to pay for." "This will be the last year until we retire." "We will remain healthy for one more year." It was always the same toast to "One more year," and they never had to explain what they meant to each other or anyone else.

One year during the anniversary dinner when their daughter had joined them, they made the same toast to "One more year."

Her daughter had asked her, "Mom, why have you put up with him all these years?" joking right in front of her dad.

She had thought about it for a minute and said, "Because I was always afraid that if I left, I would miss something fun." She had meant it. She loved this old fart and didn't know what life without him would be like, but she knew it wouldn't be the same.

They had tough times—the death of their son, raising her husband's little sister when his parents could not, supporting his mother when she was tossed out on the street by his drunken father, the long cancer battle with her mother and not being able to afford any help. They had held it together through all that and still managed to have fun in between all that sadness.

Those were the bad times, but the happy times far outnumbered the unhappy ones.

"We'll get through this too, baby," she said and patted his hand. She got a brush off the counter and brushed his hair lovingly. "That's better."

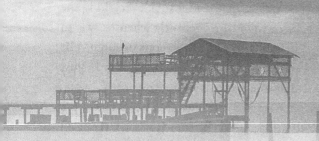

CHAPTER 4

As the sun continues to grow hotter and rise higher in the sky on this pier, I find myself thinking of some of the early summers at the camp. The early days, which in reality would have been in the early 1970s, were times to brag about the water of Mobile Bay. The water was clear but not quite as blue or greenish blue as the Gulf of Mexico. The water of Mobile Bay was brackish water, which is a mixture of both fresh water and salt water. The mixture causes the water to be a different color than the clear gulf water, but it was still clear. It was never the crystal clear water of the Caribbean but more the color of weak ice tea. The bay in the early '70s was teeming with fish and crabs. People were excited to jump in the water and take their kids.

In the early 1970s, the best thing about the camp was the easy access to the seafood. I grew up on the Mobile side or the west side of Mobile Bay close to Dauphin Island. Mobile Bay is a horseshoe-shaped bay. The west side is more populated city, and the east side, which was called the Eastern Shore, was rural farmland. The two southern ends of the horseshoe are an opening of only three miles wide. On the west side of this passage into Mobile Bay was Fort Gaines, and on the east side of the passage was Fort Morgan. Both of these were Confederate forts that protected the bay from invasion during several memorable civil war conflicts, the most well-known was the Battle of Mobile Bay. You can google it, but it was fairly uneventful unless you grew up around here. The most famous was the invasion by General Farragut, when he yelled the famous "Damn the torpedoes! Full speed ahead!" as both Fort Gaines and Fort Morgan shot everything they had at the opposing forces who were entering the bay to take over the port of Mobile.

I grew up on this body of water and always loved the seafood that it provided us. One of my first jobs when I was just eight years old was crabbing. Mobile Bay has blue claw crabs, and as early as I can remember, they were always a favorite of mine. My buddy Alvin Kennedy and I would walk down to the beach behind my house in Mobile after school, and we would run the crab traps, which meant that we would get the crabs out. Then we would bait the traps with more raw chicken necks and other leftovers from our mothers' kitchens so that we would have more crabs the next day. Crabs are bottom-feeders and eat anything dead or dying, so whatever we could get to put in those traps worked. Some days we had time after school to throw cast nets and get fish that we could use as bait.

This was actually a fairly good moneymaking venture for a couple of middle school kids. We were able to sell our crabs to the friends of our parents at first. Then we made contacts with a local store, and they would buy everything they could get.

Once we mastered the art of crabbing, we were able to step up to the next level of seafood harvesting with our profits. The local seafood store would pay dearly for any soft-shell crabs that we could find, and this was our specialty. Alvin and I had learned to read the signs of the moon and weather to know, even as small children, when was the most likely time that the crabs would be shedding their shells to grow bigger shells. During this shedding process, you had to be quick to get to the crabs and get them on ice before the shells started to harden again. The local seafood market paid a good price for soft-shell crabs, and we made a killing on them.

Once we had saved enough money from the crab trap harvest, we purchased a used, somewhat holey twenty-foot mullet net. We were barely tall enough to keep from drowning as we pulled the small net back and forth across the shallows of the bay—Alvin on one end and me on the other, both going around in circles just off the beach. The trick was to encircle the fish and anything else inside the net as we closed the two ends together. The process is not a difficult one. You both walk out several yards off the beach. Then one person takes his end and circles back toward the other person, trapping the fish in the middle. We were amazed every day at the things we would catch. The best catch was the mullet, but we took striped bass, crabs, flounder, and occasionally a small sand shark. It was all good to the fish market, and we were able to sell almost everything we caught. We did a good job of making sure that both of our families ate well from our harvest too. What our moms didn't want to cook we had a ready market for in the neighborhood if the seafood market didn't purchase it. Plenty of people wanted to buy our fish. We were rich by a kid's standards. Anything left over that was not edible was recycled into the crab traps as bait.

It's great to sit here on this pier and look across the bay at Dauphin Island and think about those days. That was good clean fun for us kids, and it taught us a lot about business. With the money I made, I was able to buy my girlfriend at the time, who later became my wife, a pearl ring that she still wears to this day. Alvin and I were able to pay to take our dates to movies at the theater or the football games. We learned early the value of money and that working hard paid off. Alvin became a master plumber after high school and did very well for himself. He died too early, in his early thirties, but he was a hardworking man with good values until the end.

Crabs aren't the only seafood we take from Mobile Bay. The oyster fishing was amazing in the '60s and '70s. This was before the state of Alabama killed the Mobile Bay reefs. We always had an ample supply of oysters in the bay until the Department of Public Transportation built up the causeway in the early '70s and the Bayway in 1978, both of which connect the east side of Mobile Bay with the west side. In an attempt to save money, the state had dredged the bay by raking all the oyster reefs, which were full of oyster shells, to build the Bayway. The oysters are natural filters for the water, and when the state of Alabama dredged these oyster reefs, they eliminated the filters. The environmentalist at the time said that the reefs would come back, but as with everything in the environment, we didn't know for years the actual effect of their actions. The oyster reefs never did come back, and twenty years later none of the same people who made those decisions were in office to hold accountable. By eliminating the oyster beds, they eliminated the filters and caused the water to become the darker, muddy color that it is today.

In the late '70s, we would spend a couple of hours in a seventeen-foot aluminum boat with oyster tongs, swoop up the delicious treats, and return to the dock with a potato sack full of oysters. My friend Joe "Chubby" Boykin and I would go out around six in the morning and be back before breakfast with so many oysters that our fingers would be bloody and swollen by noon from shucking and cleaning all of them.

If my father-in-law, Eric, was there, the three of us would stand at the end of this pier with oyster knives in one of our hands and beers in the others, laughing and telling lies about times when we were teenagers while his wife and mine kept the children busy and away from us so that they wouldn't hear all the tales. Like cleaning crabs, cleaning oysters requires a lot of self-restraint so that you don't eat them as you clean them. One of the women would always take pity on us and bring us a sleeve of saltines and a mixture of catsup and horseradish for our catch while we cleaned them. After we had eaten as many as we could stomach, my lovely wife would fry up the remaining oysters for dinner with the kids. We were fairly lucky that the kids did not decide for many years that the ugly little creatures that looked too slimy to eat where actually delicious. Many a cold beer from Dad's ice chest was consumed in the process of cleaning fish, crabs, and oysters on the end of this pier. And many a friendship was cemented for life with those smelly, cut-up hands.

My best friend for my life, he is more like a brother to me than a friend. His name is Mark Cramton, but he had always been known as Silver Dollar. I had supported Mark through three marriages and two divorces. He had supported me through so many personal crises, too many to count. During the worst day of my life, when my son died, it was Mark who went to identify my son's body when he was found. I can't imagine the strength that took. Mark was like a second father to Danny. Mark was there when Danny drank his first beer. He was there when Danny went to the University of Alabama, and he was there when I had my first heart attack. Mark only had daughters, so Danny was the son he never had.

When I had my first heart attack, Mark's wife, Barbara Dee, had immediately come to the hospital in Mobile to sit with my wife during the surgery. My wife had told them that she didn't want anybody there, so Barbara Dee, who was a nurse, sneaked into the waiting room and sat on the other side of the room, hiding from my wife's view. Once the surgery was over and my daughter had arrived from Maine, Barbara sat listening to the doctors. It wasn't until my daughter saw her that my wife even knew she was there. Barbara was that way. She was always there for my family, always willing to answer questions and give medical counsel when we needed it. She is our angel.

Mark, on the other hand, is the opposite. Mark was the one who smuggled a cold beer into the hospital when they finally put me in a room. It was Mark who picked me up from the hospital after the heart attack to drive me home. My wife had missed a lot of work, so Mark volunteered to help, but she made us promise that we would go straight home. A few hours after my release, she had called the house to see how I was doing, but we weren't there. This was before everyone had cell phones attached to themselves all the time, so she had no way of finding us.

I had gotten in Mark's car after my release for the hospital, and he had asked, "Where to, Coon?" Coon was my nickname. I think it was short for Calhoun. But Mark said it one day, and it stuck. My wife is Momma Coon, and my daughter is Baby Coon. These all came from the hunting camp and Mark.

When Mark asked, "Where to, Coon?" I responded, "Let's get a beer."

"No problem," Mark answered. And we drove to Trader John's, a bar on the Bayway between Mobile and Fairhope. This was one of our favorite places to hide out as it was a little out of the way of normal traffic and nobody really looked for us there. We had a couple of beers. I showed the bartender and a couple of the patrons my scars from the surgery, which earned me a free beer. Before we knew it, the time had gotten away from us, and it was time for my wife to get home. We hurried home, but she was steaming! She is a cute little thing, only five feet tall, but she can take you down with a look.

Mark and I were always getting into trouble like that. It caused a rift between my wife and Mark. There were times when they didn't talk for weeks at a time. My wife blamed Mark for a lot of things that were my ideas, but I think she told herself that I wasn't capable of such mischief. She has spent a great deal of her life mad at Mark for all the trouble we got into. Most of time she knew it was my fault, but she loved me, and it was easier to place the blame on Mark.

Mark and I had a group of friends who rode motorcycles. We would take overnight trips to Florida for no other purpose than to just ride. It was on one of these trips with Dennis Kearney, a friend and rider, that I noticed that Mark seemed usually quiet. Mark was an outgoing guy. He always had a funny story and baited others with his humor. On this trip he seemed to be more into his own thoughts, which was unusual for him. I asked Mark a couple of times if everything was okay and he said it was without any additional comments. This went on when we stopped for lunch and again when we stopped for gas. It was totally out of character for Mark. He was generally the center of attention, a talkative and outgoing guy.

Finally, over dinner Dennis said, "Damn it, Cramton! What's going on? Something's not right with you today." After staring at his feet for a while, Mark explained that he had a job offer in Ohio. It was a really good offer, and he would be making a lot more money. The benefits were great, and he would be able to do things for his family that he would probably not be able to afford to do here in Alabama. He said the guys who interviewed him were great and his new boss seemed like a fantastic guy. Mark explained that everything logically told him to take the job and move to Ohio. And then he asked what we thought.

Dennis is a logical business-minded man. He explained to Mark that he should take the job. The money was right, and the benefits of taking this job would move his career forward faster than staying in Alabama. He said that after a few years, he could come back to Alabama and have his boss's job. He said that if it was him, he'd call the guy right now and accept the new job.

Mark was shaking his head the whole time. Dennis was right. Everything he said was right.

I sat quietly, listening to all the reasons and the justification. Mark then looked at me and asked, "Coon, what do you think?"

I looked him straight in the eye and said, "Fuck no, I wouldn't move to Ohio!"

That was the last time that we ever discussed it, and Mark didn't take the job. I didn't give any reasons. I just gave him the understanding and confirmation of what he already knew, and that was that he didn't want to move to Ohio and that was okay. Mark knew that it wasn't all about the money. It's not all about the things that you have and the possessions that you collect. At the end of the day, the thing that has connected us all these years is that understanding of what we both value. We both made a lot of decisions over the years that did have to do with money and things, but at the end, those are the decisions that we both regretted the most.

Mark has been here for me for more than fifty years. We are family. We are brothers. Not only in the sense of a relationship, but we are Mason brothers. With the basic principles of the Mason being to make better men out of good men, I believe we both have been working on this our entire lives. Sometimes it was harder than others, but it's the journey, not the destination that matters. Neither of us is perfect, but we believe in judging people on their characters, improving our moral and spiritual outlook, and broadening our mental horizons. We are brothers in every sense of the word except for our blood, and that really has never mattered to either of us.

I also have another brother in Bryon McKinley. I met Mac when we still lived in Mobile and I was working three jobs, one of which was at Rankin Printing. Mac was a single guy then, and I was newly married with one kid and another on the way. When I started in printing, Mac had spent a lot of time helping me learn the business and just being a friend. We worked together for several years; however, the printing industry took a downturn, and they needed to lay off a pressman. I was the last to be hired, so I was at the top of the list of layoffs. I knew I was at the top of the list, and so did everyone else.

I was scared to death. How were we going to make it? How was I going to pay our rent and continue to feed my family? We were so poor back then that I was delivering newspapers before I went to my job at the printing company and working to fish or cut grass in the afternoons. But the job at Rankin was the majority of our income. When I was laid off from that job, I had no idea what I would do to replace that income. I had my wife, my little sister, and soon-to-be two kids to provide for on a daily basis. My wife and I were worried that we would need to ask for more help from her parents. By this time, her mother had been helping support us with food and money.

I went into work one day, expecting it to be my last day. It was payday and a Friday. That was always the day that they got people off the payroll. When the boss came around to give out checks, he handed me mine but didn't say anything about coming to his office. The way they generally got rid of people was to call you to his office. My wife drove to Rankin at lunch to pick up my check, so we could buy groceries. We were very literarily living paycheck to paycheck. She asked what had happened, and I said, "Nothing." They had not called me to the office. After I gave her my check, I went to look for Mac. Maybe he knew something. But Mac wasn't there. I asked around, and nobody knew where he had gone. The supervisor came through at the end of the day, and I asked if he knew where Mac was.

"Yeah, he quit," said the supervisor, walking away to another task.

I was floored. When I got home that night, I called Mac immediately. He said that he had decided that he wanted to move to the eastern shore and that Rankin just wasn't his future. That was what he said, but what I knew was that being the brother he was, he had made the decision to leave the company so that I could have the position and wouldn't be laid off. As Masons, we pledged to offer assistance to every member or his family if it was requested. Mac had done this without me even asking. Mac lived the principles of charity for others. It was a decision that was bigger than I would have ever asked or expected. This guy gave up his own security for my family. He had done more for me and my family than my own father would ever have done. My wife and I were amazed and surprised that he had done it, but years later I realized that he was more than a friend and more than a Mason. He was a brother in the truest sense of the word.

Mac continued to play a huge role in my career. When he left Rankin, he moved to Poser Business Forms in Fairhope. Years later he would give me a call to let me know about a job at Poser, and that was the beginning of my time there and my movement into a management role. Mac has always been a mentor, and over the years I've turned to him for wisdom and counsel many times.

CHAPTER 5

"Yes, ma'am, I understand that this is all very confusing," said the thirty-year-old doctor standing in the hospital room before the woman. "The test showed that the cumulative effect of the stress on the heart has just become too much to keep the other vital organs functioning." The doctor paused and rubbed his head. "We are not sure of the timing of this situation or where this is all going. We may see a small recovery, but you need to prepare yourself that he may not. We just don't know at this point until the remaining blood work and test results are processed."

She stared into this young man's eyes. Only half of what was being said was actually getting through to her brain, and she understood that. It seems that she had heard the diagnosis like a hundred times over the past few months. She had listened to doctors, nurses, surgeons, and friends tell her different things. She had searched the internet for explanations of every term they told her. But the one phrase that she and her husband had focused on was "There is nothing else we can do."

Blah, blah, blah, she thought, reminding herself not to reach over and grab this guy in the white coat by the lapel and shake him, yelling, "But you don't understand how important this person is to me! This is not a patient! This is my husband, and he is my *whole life*!"

What she did instead was say, "Thank you for everything you are doing."

The young man in the white coat turned in his light blue Crocs and walked out of the hospital room and down the hall. She watched as he walked into another room that probably held another family who thought that their situation should be the only thing that this young man was focused on for the day. She reminded herself that these doctors were busy. They saw this all the time.

She walked across the room back to the chair that had been both a place to sit and a place to sleep intermittently over the past several months. She had spent a great deal of time in Thomas Hospital over the last twelve months, not as a patient but as an observer. The hospital was a place of winding hallways and confusing conversations. She had learned more about heart procedures and medications than she ever wanted to know. All she could think of now was how tired she was. For the millionth time, she reached over and held the hand lying on the clean white sheet.

A spring bouquet of flowers had been delivered by the nurse Jennifer while the doctor was talking, and she had not had time to read the card. She walked over to the arrangement and opened the small white envelope that stuck out of the baby's breath. It was from her nephew, her brother Jim's son. She had called Donnie, her nephew, earlier in the day to update him on the situation. He lived in Chicago, and it would take him days to get here if he wanted to start making plans just in case.

The flower arrangement made her laugh. She remembered a story about her husband and her brother when they were kids and working for a nursery. They had both been in their teens. The nursery had been their first real job, and they had gone to work for Flowerwood Nursery. As teenagers, they needed money, and neither of them received any money by their parents because they simply did not have money to give. The boys worked in the heat and the dirt afternoons and weekends on the fifty-acre nursery. Flowerwood had grown over the last forty years and now had multiple locations, but back then it was a family-owned business that employed several young teenagers to do the manual labor. At that time Flowerwood was considered a pretty good job for a teenager. They were paid a fair wage, and the family treated them well.

Her husband and her brother were called water boys. This was before Flowerwood had an automated sprinkler system like they have now that rolls slowly around the property and takes care of the daily watering. There was no such luxury back then, so the water boys spent hours walking between the lines of product, watering the massive rows of plants and flowers with buckets of water. One of the jobs they did was to put a tablespoon of fertilizer in each plant. The plants were in one-gallon containers, and there were endless rows of them. My brother Jim noticed that it seemed to take my husband longer to do a row of plants than it did for him. So he decided to watch and find out why it was taking him so long.

Some of the plants that were mixed in with the healthy plants had died, and Jim noticed that my husband took longer on the dead plants than on the live ones. As Jim watched, he noticed that my husband would put two tablespoons of fertilizer in the dead plants. They had been instructed to only put one tablespoon in the plants. Jim told me that he asked my husband what the heck he was doing putting two tablespoons in the dead plants. My young and naive future husband quickly explained that he was trying to bring the plants back to life. Jim thought this was a sound idea, and they both continued the practice. None of the plants came back to life. Eventually, the manager noticed what they were doing, and they were made to stop.

The woman smiled and squeezed the hand on the bed. "You have always been the optimist. Please don't give up now. Yes, I know you have worked so hard for so long. Now is a good time to get a little rest."

CHAPTER 6

From this pier I have watched a lot of changes. I think that the biggest changes have been my two kids. My wife and I were lucky enough to have two fairly decent kids who thought we were okay most of the time. Both kids loved growing up at the camp, which is now known as the beach house. It went from being a camp to a beach house when we finally moved the trailer to the back of the lot and built a two-bedroom house with a bigger sleeping porch. We also expanded from the one-butt kitchen to a real kitchen, a breakfast area, two sitting areas for watching TV, and a large screened-in seating area on the front of the house. At one point we even had a hot tub on the screened-in porch. This turned out to be an impractical use of space at a beach house, and we got rid of it after several years.

Both the kids learned to fish and crab with their grandfather on this pier. They had been given their first crab nets by Eric when they were six and seven years old. The kids had the old-style crab nets where you tied a piece of string to the wire rim that held the netting in three places. The kids held on to the end of the string that reached up to the pier. When the crab walked into the net, they quickly pulled the string, trapping the crab. The only incentive for the crab to wander into the net was a chicken neck given to them by their mother. My wife is a world-class fried chicken cook, and she always saved the chicken necks for the kids. My daughter and son would lie on their stomachs for hours on the deck of the pier with their heads and arms hanging over the side of the wood, waiting for a crab to walk into the net. When they finally had a crab in the net, they would scream and pull the net to the deck of the pier. Once the net was on the deck, the crab had a split second to consider his predicament and run either off the side of the pier or quickly slip between the boards and back into the water for safety. The kids would be screeching the entire time. It was only about half the time that they actually got the crab in the bucket.

It was always a battle between the kids who was going to hold the string first and for how long. Many screaming matches broke out when one kid thought the other was hogging the string-holding duties for too long. My wife would immediately end any of these battles of wills with the simple phrase "Keep it up, and the crab net goes into the shed!" She has always been a master negotiator. I always thought that if the US government needed somebody to solve the Middle East crisis, my wife was available. We eventually bought several crab nets to save any family bloodshed. She ruled the house now and always with tough love. We didn't baby the kids like many do today. The kids grew up and learned by making their own mistakes and paying the consequences for those mistakes. We didn't cover up what our kids did and always listened when we heard anything about their friends. It wasn't necessary to manage their teachers, friends, sports, and lives like a lot of parents do today. If they wanted something, the kids worked for it just like my wife and I had both done. We didn't have money to spoil them, so they learned to play outside and make their own fun.

Though both kids thought that their grandfather was the master fisherman of the world, I was actually the one who took them floundering. My son was eight and my daughter was not yet seven the first time I allowed them to talk me into taking them floundering with me. Fishing for flounder in Mobile Bay was not as easy as one might think. This was the late '60s, and we still used the flounder lights, which were large round reflectors that ran on propane. They were bright and hotter than hell, and they had little mesh netting that caught fire and burned. They were not safe, but they were all we had at the time. Nobody had waterproof lights back then. We used a gig, which was a broomstick with a pronged six-inch fork on the end for spearing the fish. Between the sharp gig, the burning hot light, and the fact that this fishing was done at night as we walked through the water, it was not a safe activity for a first- or second-grader to do alone. And if we were doing it today with kids this young, somebody would probably report us to the authorities for child endangerment.

We couldn't afford a modern flounder net back then, so the process of floundering was to walk along the shoreline in thigh-high water at night, holding the flounder light, which was waiting to burn you like a welding torch, with an aluminum bucket tied on a rope around your waist and a gig in the other hand. The rope connecting the bucket to you was approximately six feet long, so once the rope was tied to you, the bucket trailed behind you about three feet to keep it out of the way of your gigging the fish.

In my case, I had two kids who were six and seven years old holding on to the rope that was tied to my waist. So here we were, dragging two kids and a bucket while holding a very hot propane torch in one hand and a very sharp spear in the other. Did I mention that it was very dark and you could only see a circle of about six feet around you? Now that I think about it, we were full-on crazy to do this.

Once I spotted a flounder, I would spear the fish with the gig and try to get the flopping slippery fish into the bucket without stabbing the kids with the spear or burning any of us with the propane torch. It is amazing to think of this now and how lucky we were that our kids weren't permanently scarred. It was several years before I would teach the kids not to squeal every time we saw a fish. They also had to learn not to jump up and down when we got a fish because that just scared the other fish away. Teaching the kids to flounder was more work, and we caught a lot less fish when they were with me. The good news was that they would only be interested for a few minutes, and then I could take them back to the house and continue on by myself.

It is a miracle from God that I didn't kill them both when they were just children. It was a different time. Today kids wear helmets and kneepads for everything. They play inside more than outside. Back then kids played outside until the sun went down, and then they came inside. TV was limited to one or two hours after they had done their homework and taken their baths. The only games to play were board games. There were no electronic games for their generation. We didn't worry as much about protecting them from everything. They got tougher and learned when something hurt. They learned logic and situational analysis in order not to get hurt a second time. They were not the overly parented kids we have today. It didn't take an electronic calendar to keep up with them either. They belonged to clubs for school; however, they were limited to what they could get themselves to, and most of the time, they walked to school or to a bus.

But let's back to the fish. Once the damn fish was in the bucket, all three of us would stand there and look at our prize for several minutes while we guessed—generally incorrectly—at the weight and the size of the fish. The kids were barely tall enough to see over the edge of the bucket. My daughter, who was always short for her age, had to bounce up and down the whole time in the water just to keep her face above the water. She was like a small blonde Tigger from Christopher Robins, her head bouncing up and down to see what was happening.

Fishing with my kids was a great time. They were so naive about life and so innocent in their pure joy of the moment. The joy I saw in their eyes from these experiences was worth all the work and worry of daily life. With one bouncing up and down and the other splashing about madly at the excitement of it all, it is a mystery we ever caught the second fish. But it seemed that we always did, and there was always plenty to fry for the next day's meal.

My son, Danny, took to the water and everything about the camp immediately. He and his best friend Joey could not get enough of the place. When Danny was twelve, his grandfather bought an aluminum boat and a fifteen-horsepower battery-powered motor. The two boys spent every weekend running the small seventeen-foot boat up and down the beach in front of our house. Every night we plugged that little motor in to recharge it, and by lunchtime the next day, it was dead as a doornail again. The pure joy of a boy and a boat was a sight to see. It gave the boys a lot of freedom to fish other parts of the coast. It gave them the skills to manage the boat and learn the currents and weather. It may have only been a seventeen-foot craft; however, they were learning captaining skills, and there was a lot to be said for that. Of course, we had rules about how deep they could go and how far away they were allowed, but as time passed and the trust was built, they wandered farther away on these adventures.

The problem with owning the small boat did not start until my little girl was twelve and developed a need to compete with her older brother over everything. The screaming matches over who was going to hold the string to the crab trap was nothing compared to the fights over the small boat. If it was just my two kids, they were fine. If either of them had friends down, they could get along and go in the boat together. The problem was when either one of them had a friend at the beach. Because Danny and Joey were boys and older, they thought they had an inherent right to the craft. The last thing either of the thirteen-year-old boys wanted on the boat was a girl. So my baby girl often got left on the beach, which made her madder than you could imagine, madder than a sweet little toe-headed blonde could be.

One weekend when Danny and Joey were thirteen and my daughter was eleven, she had a friend down for the weekend. The normal argument started over the boat that Saturday morning. The boys wanted the boat to go fishing, and the girls wanted the boat primarily to keep it away from the boys. My wife heard the argument in the front yard, and without leaving the trailer, the master negotiator yelled, "I'll put the damn boat in the backyard, and nobody will use it if I hear one more word!" After a much quieter discussion, a consensus was reached. The girls could ride in the boat with the boys down the shoreline to a little inlet where the guys wanted to fish. The girls could lie in the sun, and the boys would fish. The kids were gone for several hours when I walked out to the end of the pier and looked down the beach, wondering where they were. Several hundred yards down the beach, I saw two kids walking up the beach toward our pier. When they got close enough, I realized that it was Danny and Joey.

I met the boys on the opposite side of Obie's property and asked where the boat and the girls were. The boys explained that the battery had run out on the motor. The boys had rowed the boat for a ways, arguing with the girls the whole time that they needed to help row the boat. The girls had refused to row the boat, claiming that it wasn't their idea to go down to the inlet to fish so they should not have to help row the boat. When the current changed and the tide began to go out, the boys decided to get out of the boat and swim to the shore. They said they told the girls to get out and swim. The boys claimed that they couldn't tow the boat with the girls in it. The girls didn't want to get in the water because they were afraid of jellyfish. So the girls started to row, and the boys swam to the shore. The current was picking up and the girls were slowly drifting out to the Gulf of Mexico.

In the boys' defense, the girls were only twenty yards off the beach in less than five feet of water when the boys jumped overboard. All four kids were strong swimmers and could have easily towed the boat to shore if they had worked together.

Of course, this is a decision that an adult would have made but not four teenagers who were more concerned about winning a silly power struggle over a favorite toy than doing the right and safe thing. The girls stubbornly stayed in the boat, which was quickly moving out deeper with the outgoing tide. The boys swam to shore, laughing and pointing at the girls for several minutes until they realized that the boat was headed toward the mouth of Mobile Bay. Then they walked back to the pier, understanding that everyone was probably in big trouble.

Once I got the abbreviated version of the story when I met the boys on the beach, I ran as fast as possible down the beach and swam for my life out to the boat, which was now two hundred yards off the shore with the two girls in it. I yelled at the girls to get out of the boat and start to swim. I was completely exhausted when I finally got to the boat. It was everything that I could do to hang on to the back of the boat and push a little as the girls swam in and towed the boat to shore.

My reaction to my son's behavior was total fury. By the time I got back to the house with the girls and the boat, I had reached the decision that Danny must understand that he needed to protect his little sister and that this behavior would not go unpunished. In those days, you could still whip your kids, and you bet your ass Danny got a good whipping for that stunt.

My daughter tried to take responsibility for the incident to save her brother. It was amazing how the two of them would fight like grizzly bears one minute and then defend each other the next minute. The boat was restricted to shore for several weeks, but the silver lining to that incident was that I don't remember a time when my son wasn't watching out for his sister's safety again, even when he looked uncool to his friends.

Chapter 7

The sound of fast-paced footsteps echoed down the tile hallway of the second floor of Thomas Hospital. The footsteps stopped in front of the door, and the lady sitting inside looked up to see who it was, knowing full well exactly who it would be. Finally.

"Mom?" said a whispered voice from the slightly opened door.

"Yes, baby. Come on in," the woman had been sitting with most of the lights off for some time now. She had hoped that she would be able to close her eyes for a minute and get a little sleep. She needed to sleep. It had been a long time since she had gotten a good night's sleep. She looked at her watch and was surprised that it is only ten o'clock in the morning. *Wow, I've been sitting here for four hours. It seemed like days.*

"What happened this time, Mom?" asked her daughter. She loved this kid, but even more importantly, she liked the woman this girl had become. Her daughter, who was now more than fifty years old, was still her baby girl but also her friend. She knew her daughter had been on the plane for more than twenty-six hours just to get here. She wanted to ask her about her flight, her trip, if she was tired. But she knew that there was no putting off this conversation.

Where to start? She really didn't know. She began with waking up and finding her husband with labored breathing and chest pains. She had called 911 and followed the ambulance the few short blocks from her home to the hospital. She explained to her daughter about the conversation with the emergency room doctors and then the surgeon, who looked like he was thirty years old, and the kidney specialist, who kept saying there was nothing they could do. She gave her daughter the condensed version of what the nurses were saying.

"Mom, what are you telling me?" asked her daughter, who was very perceptive and knew that her mother never told her everything. Not because she didn't want to but because she knew that her daughter, who had a good business mind, didn't handle family issues as easily, especially when it came to her father.

She looked over at the beautiful sleeping face on the pillow in the bed. She bent down and kissed her husband's forehead and said to her daughter, "Let's take a walk, okay?"

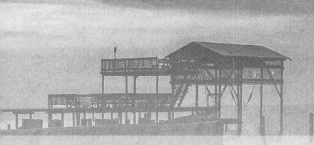

CHAPTER 8

I met the love of my life, Jackie Neumann, when my family moved from Hattiesburg, Mississippi, to Mobile, Alabama. She was a sweet little Bible thumper who spent more time at church than any kid should. We both lived in the same neighborhood and knew each other since I was eight and she was seven years old. I became quick friends with her brother Jimmy, who was my age, and we played Little League baseball on the same team. Initially, my attraction was to her slightly older friend Sue Davis. Sue had long blonde hair and a bubbly personality. I had spent a fair amount of time having Sunday dinner with her family after church. But it only took a couple of times around this quiet girl Jackie, and I was hooked. She was sweet and cared about people. Over the years she would become very independent, but as a kid, she was quiet and unassuming. She was not a girly girl—all giggly and silly like most girls her age. She was smart but kind, interested in doing things with the boys and not afraid of anything it seemed.

The Neumann family members were Southern Baptists, and it seemed that every time the doors of the church were open, they were there. When I met Jackie, the first thing I noticed was that she carried a Bible everywhere she went—to school, to play, to church. My family was not Southern Baptist. In fact, we were not really of any religion. The first time I saw my father in or around a church was when Jackie and I got married. And I'm telling you he looked damned uncomfortable that day. It may have been that he wasn't sober and that was enough to make him look that way. Being drunk was his natural state, so for him to be drunk on my wedding day was no deviation from his normal.

When we first got married, we were so young that most of the people our age in the church still lived at home. I was eighteen, and Jackie was sixteen. We were the first of our social group to get married and have our own place, so all the young people in the church hung out at our house on weekends. It was always fun. We were kids and happy just to have friends and a place to hang out away from the real adults. It was innocent fun. We told jokes and laughed for hours. All our friends were Southern Baptist, so none of our group drank, of course. Once the jokes had run out and everyone got quiet, my brother-in-law Jimmy made a new rule. The rule was that if you weren't laughing, you had to throw money into a cup in the middle of the coffee table. Well, none of us had any money, so the jokes rolled on and on.

We were poor, we were young, and we were struggling, but we were happy. I think that we didn't really know what poor was back then. With friends and family around us, it sure seemed that we were a couple of the happiest people we knew. We lived in a small house about three miles away from Jackie's parents, so they kept a close eye on us, and once the kids started coming, they kept a closer eye on the grandbabies.

My family had moved from Hattiesburg for my father's new job. My father had a lot of *new* jobs over a short period of time, and we moved a lot during my preteen years. I was too young at the time to know why my father had so many jobs, but it didn't take me many years to figure out that the drinking had a lot to do with it. Most of the moves were around Hattiesburg. I believe that he exhausted his resources around Mississippi and that was why we had to relocate to Mobile, Alabama.

My father was a man to watch when you lived with him. You never knew how much he was going to drink, and when he drank, you wanted to stay away from him. Most of the time, my dad was a fairly entertaining drunk, but it only took a little something like my mother's opinion to change that funny drunk into a mean drunk. The mean drunk in him would strike like a rattlesnake in the dark.

My mother, a small woman who was less than five feet tall, was the target of most of his meanness when we were small kids. I had a sister who was seven years younger than me, and we learned early to stay out of the way when we were kids. By the time I grew into my teenage years, I spent a lot of time stepping in front of my mother, which meant that rattlesnake made me his target. That lasted until I was old enough to learn that I could hit back and get away with it. As long as he was drunk enough, he didn't remember me fighting back to stop him.

About two months after we got married, we moved my then ten-year-old sister in with us. I was eighteen years old and already the man responsible for my sixteen-year-old wife and my ten-year-old sister. My son would follow eighteen months later and my daughter sixteen months after that. So at twenty-one years old, I was responsible for four other human beings.

My father had gotten worse by then, and my mother had moved out of his house and back to Mississippi to escape him. He had followed her back to Mississippi, although they never lived together again. I had made every effort to keep this man away from my wife, my sister, and later my kids. By the time I had my son, I was getting regular phone calls from the Mississippi State Police reporting my father's misadventures.

One night around midnight, I received a phone call from the state police in Mississippi. They explained that my father was standing on a bridge over the Mississippi River and that he was threatening to jump. They suggested that I come quickly. I told them I would not. Then they asked me what they should say to my father. "He is asking for you," they said. "What should we say to him?"

Without a second thought, with no emotions, no regrets, and no concern, I told the Mississippi state police officer, "Tell him to jump." That may sound harsh, but by this time I had bailed this man, who was my father but no one's dad, out of jail so many times that I could not afford to continue to support his daughter and my children and pay his bail. I had given up on him and didn't want anything to do with the shell of a person who had been my father. He had never been a role model or even someone who cared about his family. He had been a drunk from the time he was able to make decisions about drinking. He was one person who should never have had a family, and he definitely didn't deserve to keep the one he did have.

I take only a moment to wonder what the infamous John Calhoun would say about his son now. I'm sitting here on the end of this pier, a man successful beyond my father's dreams, looking at the beauty of nature that he could never have appreciated through his haze of booze. I have a great family and friends who would do anything in the world just to make me smile. He never knew that kind of love and never deserved that kind of respect.

I was raised by a woman who was the housekeeper for my grandfather and grandmother. Nettie Mae was a black woman who made sure that I knew right from wrong. She was the strongest female in my life until I met my wife. She nursed my mother physically when I couldn't, but she could never fix my mother's emotional pain. No one could fix that. Her mother and grandmother had also worked for my mother's family before her. Nettie's house, which was actually my grandparents' house, was the safe haven where my sister and I were taken when Dad got out of control. Nettie's house was a huge antebellum home in old Hattiesburg. It always smelled like ham and pecan pie. No matter what the day of the week or the time of the year, that was the smell. She was my saving grace and a mentor to the kindness in life I wanted and ultimately would live. Nettie lived in peace. She showed respect for those who earned it and tolerance for those who didn't.

She was a religious woman but not a judgmental one. When she was young, she would take care of the house and the family. She did everything from cut wood for the woodstove to wax the floors once a week. Everything in the house revolved around her without anyone knowing it. She commanded the house and the family but allowed my grandfather to believe that he was in charge.

It was from this woman in the '50s and '60 that I learned what it meant to be a good man. She never raised her voice except to scream, "Praise God!" when something good happened. She gave me books she bought from her small hourly wage as a maid, even though she herself never learned to read. Nettie had lived her whole life in the employ of my family, but she was never allowed to sit at the table in the formal dining room. That was the way it was in southern Mississippi at the time. But regardless, she was the most enlightened, self-confident, brilliant person I have ever known. She understood people and passed this knowledge to me. I would carry with me the lessons that I learned from this employee of my grandfather's to my family and relationships for the rest of my life.

When Nettie died more than twenty years ago, I cried like I had lost a blood relative, a family member. When my father finally died, I didn't even bother to attend the funeral. He simply went into the ground, which was as cold and black as his heart had been in life.

Chapter 9

My daughter grew up, and regardless of my efforts to keep her living nearby, she decided to move to New England to work and finish school. She had gotten her college degree, which no one else in our family had done. She went on to get her master's degree, and I'm not sure that I've ever told her how proud I was of her. When she left Alabama, it was very hard on her mother, and strangely enough, it was tough on me as well. I enjoyed being Daddy to my little girl even if she was now twenty-six years old. She was working and going to school and was only able to come home twice a year, once during the summer and once during in the winter.

One year she made the decision to come home for Thanksgiving and hunt instead of coming home for Christmas. She had a boyfriend and wanted to spend Christmas that year with his family. During her stay in the wintry Northeast, she had learned to knit to pass the long, cold days. This knitting hobby had turned into heartfelt gifts for everyone in Alabama that year. She had spent a great deal of time knitting me a sweater. I received it shortly before Christmas and opened the gift when my wife and I returned from a trip to Jamaica for the holiday. The sweater was a cardigan with a wide roll collar. She had looked long and hard to find the exact color of the University of Alabama—crimson red. She had spent God only knew how many hours handcrafting this treasure. When I unwrapped it and called to tell her thank you, we could hear the joy and pride in her voice as I told her how much I loved it.

The sweater was a mess! One sleeve was a good four inches below the ends of my fingers with my arm stretched out. The other sleeve was two inches above my wrist, which made one sleeve six inches longer that the other. When I tried to button it, the holes on the cardigan didn't line up with the buttons, causing puckers and pouches all the way up and down the front of the sweater. I looked like Mr. Rogers, but homeless and on crack. "Will you be my neighbor?" But I wore it anyway because I promised that baby girl that I would.

At the time I was working for Baldwin County, the county we live in, as the director of human resources. On the day after we returned to work from our holiday vacation, I wore my cardigan proudly to work. It just so happened that the county commission had a meeting that day, and the press were present. The press were vultures even back then and always on the hunt for a story.

When my turn came, I approached the podium professionally and confidentially to present a change in the medical insurance plan for their approval. When I had first gotten up to walk to the front room, I saw the smiles on the commissioner's face and the grinning of my peers in the gallery. However, without any explanation or apologies, I made my pitch about the value of changing our health insurance from standard indemnity plans to a health maintenance organization. I reviewed the cost-benefit analysis of the program and the added benefit to our employees. In the presentation I passionately summarized the value of preventive care coverage and the limitations to network doctors in the area. I had no idea whether anyone heard a word I said; however, they were kind, and nobody openly laughed at my sweater.

After the commission meeting had concluded their business, the county administrator, to whom I reported, came to my office and closed the door behind him. He sat in the chair across from my desk while I continued to stand behind the desk to make sure that he had a good view of my "Mr. Rogers on crack" sweater.

"Anything we need to talk about, Byron?" he asked. We were good friends as well as boss and subordinate. I understood that he must be very concerned.

"No, nothing I can think of," I said, wearing my best poker face.

"Any problems at home? Jackie doing okay?" he was obviously fishing for an explanation of why I looked the way I did. "Everything fine with the family?"

At that moment the intercom system on my desk squawked as my assistant said, "Line one, Byron. It's Donna."

"One minute," I said, holding up my index finger to my boss.

"Yes, honey," I said to my only daughter. "Good afternoon to you too. Yes, we got our presents. Yes, I got the sweater you sent. I know you made it with your own hands, baby. Of course I love it. In fact, I'm wearing it today. Yes, I told everyone that you made it yourself. Yes, they loved it, honey. I know that it is the exact color of the University of Alabama. Yes, honey, I love you too. We'll talk soon." With that, I hung up the phone and turned to look at my boss. He was looking at the window, and he had clearly been listening to the conversation.

"You were saying, Bob?" I asked.

He turned from the window, grinning from ear to ear, understanding in his eyes. When you are a dad and especially when you are a father of a daughter as he and I both are, some things defy explanation. They just are and need to be. Without saying so, he knew, and I knew he would have worn the homeless man sweater that day too. With a pat on my shoulder, he left my office, smiling, off to explain to the other commissioners that I was indeed sober and sane. The only explanation needed was it was a Christmas present from my baby girl.

Dads do a lot of things that they don't always like to do. Eat your six-year-old daughter's Shake 'N Bake cookies that taste like paste. Sit through four hours of everybody else's kids' ballet recitals to watch a three-and-a-half-minute dance by your daughter when she's seven. Sitting through countless softball games where she doesn't get to play just in case this one time she does get to walk onto the field with the rest of the team. Attending her wedding and giving her away to a guy you would rather kill than give her hand to. You do these things because you are her dad, not just her father.

"Daughters!" I say to myself as I look west toward the mouth of the bay. The breeze is warm and crisp. The sun is lower on the horizon now. "What day is this?" I asked myself, looking at my wrist where my watch should be. It seems that since I retired, I ask myself what day it is a lot. And then I remember that I don't care because I'm retired.

When I look down the deck of the pier toward the beach and the house, from this distance I can see someone on the front porch of the house that we built to replace the trailer in 1980. The front porch is a large screened-in gathering place. I can't tell who it is on the porch, but I'm sure the person will work his or her way out here soon. Visitors always do.

In the 1980s, I had been working for a large printing company for many years, and my wife and I were able to save enough money to have a true house built on the property. This was the point when the camp became the beach house. A trailer was a camp; this was a beach house. We pulled the trailer out of the way and paid to have the house roughed in by a friend of mine named Cecil Ward, who owned a construction company. The roughed-in house was a twelve-hundred-square-foot box when the contractors left the property. They put up the walls and did the electrical work. Then my wife and I spent every weekend for a year doing the finish work ourselves. In the beginning we slept in the trailer and worked every day until we were exhausted. We hung Sheetrock and ran the plumbing. Then once we had the walls up in the house, we slept on the floor on air mattresses until we got the floors down and could move in minimal furniture. We hung the cabinets, put in the fixtures, painted, and laid the carpet. We put the screen on the porch and put the decking and stairs to the house on ourselves.

We only had enough money to do a little at a time, and we committed to each other that we would never owe any money on the beach house no matter what. So every payday we would pay the *real* bills for the house in Fairhope and then decide what light fixture we would buy with what was left over. It was a long process, but doing the work together was fun. We learned a lot about each other. We laughed a lot and yelled a lot too. Now when I walk through the house, which we've renovated and added onto several times over the thirty years, I can see every touch of my wife's hand. I remember her deciding on each color for the walls and each picture I hung and every stick of furniture we bought over time.

I think that is why I think of the beach house as my wife's house and the pier as my pier. Heaven knows we have rebuilt this pier too many times to count. In 2005, we rebuilt this pier four times. That was the year that it was destroyed by Hurricane Ivan the fall of 2004, and we waited until the early spring to rebuild it. The pier was rebuilt in April because we always committed to have all the work done on the beach house by May 1 so that we could enjoy the summer. The rule was that if it wasn't done by May 1, we had to forget about it until next year. So we completed the repairs for Hurricane Ivan in April 2005. On the first week of June, the hurricane season from hell started, and the Gulf Coast got hit with a tropical storm that tore the boards from the deck of the pier and removed pieces of the roof over the attached boathouse. All rules of no work after May 1 went out the window as we rebuilt the pier again in June.

My daughter's boyfriend at the time, a great man named Harry Wilson, helped rebuild the pier, and we thought we were good for the year. Less than two months later, Hurricane Dennis traveled a path through the gulf that followed Ivan's. So the weather rolled into the coast of Alabama to destroy my pier again. Ever-vigilant, Harry and I started the physically demanding work of rebuilding the damn thing again in July. Mother Nature allowed us to keep the pier for a good three months before she decided to introduce us to the wrath of a gal named Hurricane Katrina. Harry and my daughter broke up shortly after, and he has never returned to the beach house since. He always said that the work had nothing to do with the end of their relationship, but I still feel a little guilty about that one. I really liked the guy.

My daughter had a lot of girlfriends she hung around, and one of the closest was our next-door neighbors in Fairhope. Fred and Sandra Bostrom had three girls, and my daughter was friends with them all. Being next-door neighbors, our kids spent a lot of time together, and so did their parents. We were known to walk next door with a bottle of wine for no reason, and so did they. The Bostroms had a really nice pool and screened-in back porch that was perfect for wine (or anything else) drinking. When you meet Fred, you might consider him a little snooty, but he is honestly one of the funniest guys I've ever known. Fred was a natural-born salesman. He could sell anything, and a story was the easiest sell. He has a ton of them, and he can entertain a group of people for days with his stories. Don't give too much thought to whether they are true or not. That's not important. Fred's stories are for entertainment value only.

One weekend in August, Jackie and I had been at the beach working all weekend, and we came home late from the linen service. We took our baths and got ready for bed. I lay there for a few minutes and thought I heard water running. I got up and looked in the kitchen and the other bathrooms on the other side of the house, thinking that the kids had left the water running somewhere, but there was nothing. But I could hear the water running. I was exhausted and went back to bed. I sat on the side of the bed for a minute and asked Jackie if she heard water running. She listened and said that she did. I got back up and went to the east side of the house. I checked all the water faucets but didn't see anything. I walked around the house, and finally when I got to the west side of the house, I saw that there was a hose hooked up and that the water was turned on.

I followed the hose straight over to Fred Bostrom's house. It was late, but I banged on his door anyway.

"What the hell are you doing, Bostrom?" I asked, a little pissed off.

Fred wiped his eyes. He was already in his pajamas. "Filling the pool!" he said.

"Why the hell are you using my water!" I asked.

"Because it's faster with both than just mine," he said as if I should have already figured that out myself.

Years later when they decided to move, I reminded Fred that the house might be his but that the water in the pool was mine.

CHAPTER 10

The two women were sitting in the cafeteria of the hospital and drinking coffee. Both had not touched the Danish that was in front of them.

"It is decision time," Jackie said to her daughter. "The message is clear. Dad's situation is not going to get better. The doctor said that they have done everything they can. They won't do anymore."

"What about a second opinion?" asked her daughter.

"That was the second opinion and the third," said Jackie with a slight pained smile and a pat on her daughter's hand.

"You know, I just keep thinking that they will figure it out and do something. Maybe a transplant? What about that? Has anybody said anything about a transplant?" she asked her mother.

"Not at his age, honey," Jackie said and stirred her coffee, which was now cold. "They are done. The doctors are just trying to make things as easy as they can. Believe me, I've begged and pleaded. I understand now. We are done."

Flashes from the last sixty years of her married life had been running through her mind for the last couple of days. She knew that she had been very lucky to have had a wonderful husband and great kids. There were so many memories, so many celebrations.

They had gotten married when she was only sixteen years old. It really was only three months before her seventeenth birthday, but that was a different time. People got married earlier in the 1950s than they do now. In their case, it was a necessity. Her father-in-law was out of control, and her husband and best friend needed to get out of his father's house and away from him. His little sister also needed a place to live away from the crazy father. It was the kind of wedding where everyone said, "It will never last," even though divorce was rare then. But the marriage had lasted for sixty years. It had not always been easy.

They were all gone now, all those people who had said it wouldn't last—both of her parents and both of his parents. His sister had grown up and moved away; however, she had died several years ago, and so had her brother Jimmy. Their son, Danny, had been dead for more than thirty years now. All that was left was her daughter and her husband. And now she was losing him too.

As she sat looking at the white industrial cafeteria table, she knew it was the two of them now—mother and daughter. And they needed to make decisions.

She remembered when she and her husband first started dating. Everything seemed easy then. They were so young and so in love. He was a year ahead of her and attended Theodore High School. She was a student at Murphy High School. They had lived less than a mile apart for most of their lives, but the lines for the two schools fell right between their houses. It had become impossible to keep him at Theodore during the days when he should have been at school. He spent more time at Murphy, her school, than he did at his. He was there so much that several teachers had fussed at him to get to class when he was found roaming the halls between classes. The teachers saw so much of him and the school was so large that the teachers assumed he was also a student.

Her love had been a football player for Theodore and a good one at that. Even at the age of seventeen, colleges were looking at him. She was a church organist and had talent, but that wouldn't go anywhere either. Her mother liked the boy, and her father saw some potential; however, they both understood that if this young man was going to grow up to be a decent person, he needed to get away from his rotten father. Byron was a bit of a hooligan, and Jackie was a Southern Baptist kid, so they were a bit of a mismatch. But he was in love with her, and she with him. He had given up fishing and crabbing on Sunday morning to go to their church and impress her parents.

Everyone in the neighborhood understood who and what his father was, but in the '50s, you did not discuss such things in public. He was an alcoholic who beat his wife and his kids. Jackie's mother, Merle, had been a kind and thoughtful woman who tried hard not to judge Byron's father or his mother for putting up with it. Merle had been the stability that Byron needed, and as a teenager, he had spent many a night at their house sleeping in Jimmy's room to keep him away from his drunk father. Byron loved his mother-in-law almost as much as he had loved his young bride.

Jackie couldn't really remember how the decision had been made to get married. Thinking back on it, they were standing in front of the Forest Park Bible Church with her parents when the discussion started. It seemed that the decision was more her mother's doing than either hers or Byron's. It was like her parents had decided that it was the right thing to do, and they needed to do it sooner rather than later. Byron had just finished his senior year, and she still had another year to go. But things started moving in that direction, and before either one of them knew what had happened, they were standing in front of the small Baptist church. The wedding was small with both sets of parents, the bride and groom, and only a couple of close friends from the church present. She laughed every time she looked at the wedding photo in their house in Fairhope, they both looked scared to death. His father standing two feet away from the rest of the group, her mother smiling from ear to ear next to Eric.

As she sat in the hospital cafeteria and remembered those days, she thought about how poor they had been in the beginning. They lived in a duplex apartment on the bay with her husband working three jobs. They had furnished the duplex with things they had gotten from her parents. They had slept in her bed that she had had since she was four years old. The rest of their furniture had come out of her parents' attic. They were young, and their place was cute and had a touch of home. They needed to rent a house shortly after when they knew that Suzanne needed to come to live with them. They had worked so hard for everything they had.

When they first got married, Byron had worked for Bender Welding Company; however, the contract had been canceled, and then he found the job delivering newspapers. His day started at four in the morning with the paper route. He would finish delivering papers by five forty and come back to the house and get his new bride to drop her off at Murphy High School for her last year. He would then go to his real job of running a printing press for a small family-owned printing company in downtown Mobile.

On the weekends he worked doing odd jobs, cutting grass or building fences, whatever he could find to do to make the few extra dollars they needed for rent and utilities. He had also kept up with his fishing and crabbing and regularly sold the catch at the yacht club. His sister had moved in with them, and they did their best to keep her in shoes and jeans. They had taken a short honeymoon to Biloxi and Hattiesburg to visit family, but without any money, it was a very simple trip.

She remembered that they had two cars when they first got married. To anyone who didn't know better, they would think that they were rich because only rich people had two cars. But that was not the case for them. Her husband had two cars because he had three jobs. Both cars were old and constantly breaking down. When he had problems with one car, he would borrow parts off the other car to make it to his work. Then when he had a little free time and money, he could get the second car fixed, knowing that the first car would surely break down sooner or later. It was a constant juggling act to maintain his transportation for the paper route and as a printing press operator job downtown.

When they finally got around to a real honeymoon, it was a second trip to Biloxi, Mississippi, only fifty miles away from their home, but it was a world away from their two small babies. Danny had come only eighteen months after they were married, and their daughter had come sixteen months after him. They had looked forward to the honeymoon for years, and the day had finally come. Byron had gotten the weekend off from all his jobs, and they had packed up the car with what little money they had and headed off to the beach in Biloxi for the weekend, leaving the two babies with her parents.

She remembered that they had arrived at the hotel in Biloxi around seven o'clock that Friday night. After getting their small bag with limited clothes in the room, they had gone out to dinner. This was the first dinner that either of them could remember in a restaurant where they had tablecloths on the table and real linen napkins wrapping the silverware. There were no kids screaming and demanding attention, but the kids seemed to be the only thing that they talked about that night. The next morning they woke up early, and Byron said, "I'm going to get my babies." He drove all the way back to Mobile and picked up the kids and then returned to their honeymoon with his two babies.

Merle had laughed when she answered the door and found Byron standing there, wanting the babies.

"What happened to the honeymoon?" she asked, knowing full well that they didn't need a hotel room in Biloxi to celebrate their life. They needed their little family, and that was all.

"Silly kids," was all Merle had said when she handed their two blonde babies back to him and watched him get into their beat-up used car and drive away.

That had been a long time ago. Now the mother and daughter sat in a sterile hospital cafeteria. Merle had died more than forty years ago. The kids had grown up, and now the love of her life was upstairs in a hospital room, leaving her as well.

"Hey, Mom," said her daughter, trying to break her mother's deep thoughts.

The mother jumped, startled out of her memories. "Yes, honey."

"Remember when Christopher Reeves fell off the horse?"

Her mother looked confused. "You mean Christopher Reeves that played Superman?"

"Yeah, Superman." Her daughter looked at her coffee cup. "This is a lot like that."

The mother laughed. "I'm not following you, baby."

"You take a man like Christopher Reeves, who plays Superman, and he seems unstoppable." The younger woman explained, "It wasn't that an old actor was suddenly in a wheelchair. It was Superman was now disabled.

"Just watching him on TV seemed unbelievable. People kept wondering if it was possible." Her daughter had tears in her eyes. "Dad is like that. It is as hard to believe that Dad can't pull out of this just like it was hard to believe that Superman was confined to a wheelchair."

Her mother reached across the table and held her daughter's hand. She knew that this child belonged more to her husband than she had ever belonged to her mother. This girl was a daddy's girl, even at fifty-plus years. She remembered when she had lost her own mother in her twenties, her father in her thirties, and her son in her forties. It just didn't get any easier and never made any sense at the time.

"It's just a part of life, baby," the mother finally said. "Just a part of life."

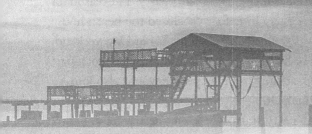

CHAPTER 11

The pier is a simple piling pier, which means that down the center of the walkway or deck to the end of the pier is only one piling in the middle. It was constructed by making a T out of the top of the piling, which gives more stability to support the base. The top of the T is connected by a V under that. We have a V with a board across the top when all is said and done. A great number of piers are actually made with a two-piling construction, but I have always believed that in a good hurricane or a heavy winter storm, the wind and waves are going to get twice as many pilings in a two-piling construction. I have noticed over the last fifty years that two-piling piers seem to lose more pilings because floating logs get in between the two pilings that are side by side and knock down the whole pier easier.

It is midday, and the sun is high in the sky. I can't see the house from here because of the cedar trees that are covered in moss, but I can see the porch. The screen on the porch is dark gray to give more shade to those sitting there, so it makes it harder to see who is up there. Because the windows on the back of the house provide a sort of backlight to the people inside, I can see people moving around inside, but I have no idea who they are.

I'm not sure what is going on, but I see more than one person up at the beach house now. It's strange because nobody has walked out here to see what I'm up to. It must be some sort of party that I forgot about. The beach house is notorious for its parties, both the ones we planned and the ones that just break out without any warning.

Several years ago we had our annual dirty T-shirt party. The reason for the party was to get one more party in before we closed the beach house after Labor Day. The party was generally planned for Labor Day weekend, if the weather permitted. Labor Day is right in the middle of the worst part of hurricane season. It was great fun, and new people would also join, so you never knew who would make it.

The annual dirty T-shirt party started when a guest wore a T-shirt with a racy comment on it to the beach house years ago. And as things go, certain people thought that they had funnier T-shirts and wanted to show them off. One thing led to another, and the dirty T-shirt party was scheduled. It really just gave everyone a good excuse to buy T-shirts with questionable comments on them and have a place to wear them. We always had prizes and more alcohol than we needed. After enough alcohol, some of the T-shirts were discarded and skinny-dipping became the entertainment.

The dirty T-shirt party was the last party of the year each year, and the adult Easter egg hunt was the first party of the year each year. As the name implies, the annual event was held on the Saturday before Easter Sunday. It was only for adults. No children were allowed, not even ours. The *eggs* were not eggs at all but miniatures of alcohol—miniatures with vodka, rum, scotch, and others—with ribbons tied around the necks of the tiny bottles. Everyone would arrive at the beach house, and the normal bar that was on the screened-in porch would be closed to all, not even a beer in sight. Instead of drinks, they were given Easter baskets and told to go find their drinks. You can imagine twenty adults running around the yard, trying to find miniatures of booze, placing them in their baskets, and running to the next miniature.

There were, of course, prizes like any Easter egg hunt would have. The miniature with the gold ribbon was a golden egg and won the person a bottle of champagne. The guest who found the most *eggs* won a case of beer. There were prizes for the different colors of ribbons that my wife had tied on. And there were prizes for the least number found and prizes for the most red ribbons or blue ribbons. There wasn't really any reason beyond making it fun.

After all the miniatures were counted to make sure that we had found all the small bottles—it was never fun to find them with the lawn mower later in the year—the trading began. It was just as entertaining watching adults begin to negotiate for the miniatures they wanted. They used the bottles they found and bargained for the booze that they really liked. If you were a vodka drinker and had three bottles of rum, you found a rum drinker who would trade you for vodka. The longer the bidding went on, the crazier the trading got. It really got interesting when you didn't have anything that another person had but still needed a drink. It was then that the bidding got very creative.

There were parties for the Fourth of July, Memorial Day, my birthday in May, spring break for the kids, my daughter's birthday in August, and everything else we could think of. We had weddings and receptions down here. There was always a reason for a party.

You never know how many friends you have until you get a place at the beach. This little pier has seen a lot of celebrations, and I've been here for most of them. The attendees have changed slightly over the years, but the usual suspects are always here.

One of the most delicious and easiest parties we ever had was the first annual chicken cook-off. It never made it to the second annual one, but not from a lack of participation in the first. The chicken cook-off started quite innocently. A friend of my daughter named Rich Edgeworth believed that he was the best grill cook in south Alabama. We had been at the beach house for a long weekend, and I had grilled my signature barbecue chicken. Everyone always loved my barbecue chicken. I simple quartered the chicken, got my four-foot-long concrete block grill hot and smoking and tossed the quarters on. After the chicken was almost done, I added my special barbecue sauce, which was cheap Kraft sauce, with everything from the spice cabinet and refrigerator thrown in. The real secret sauce was that the whole time the chicken was cooking, we were all sitting on the end of the pier or playing in the water. After you had smelled the chicken for an hour, you were so hungry that it tasted even better than you could imagine. The concrete block fireplace just added to the romance of the chicken. It was all slow-cooked to where it would fall off the bone with the slightest touch.

I bragged that it was a secret recipe, but it wasn't. It was the slow-cooking of the grill and the amount of beer everyone drank while waiting for the chicken to cook. As everyone sat eating the chicken that night, Rich called me out. He said that he could make better chicken on the grill than anyone, including me! My daughter came to the defense of my ability and told Rich he was full of shit! Nobody cooked better barbecue chicken than her dad! The battle was on.

The challenge grew from my chicken to anyone who wanted a piece of the action. What started as a cook-off between Rich and me quickly got out of control. When the day of the chicken cook-off finally came, the challenge had grown from my chicken to anyone with a grill and a recipe. We had nine different entrants to the contest, and somehow I had become a bystander. I never even had to light the grill that day. I just sat back and let these guys and gals make chicken for everyone there. We had drunk chicken, barbecue chicken, chicken with garlic sauce, and stuffed chicken breast. There was something for everyone. The winner ended up not being the best chicken but the one cooked by the cutest female contestant. It wasn't the chicken breast that won, but it was definitely a good breast that won!

The craziest and probably the most dangerous party we ever had on this pier was on Labor Day when Hurricane Juan made a surprise appearance in the Gulf of Mexico and headed straight for Mobile Bay. We had planned a Labor Day party, which can be questionable in south Alabama. There was a tropical storm in the middle of the gulf, but it wasn't forecast to come our way. We had all been watching the tropical storm Juan for several days. Once the storm appeared to be heading to Texas and not toward us, we decided to go ahead with the party. If you let a possible tropical storm change your summer plans in south Alabama, you'll never get to a good summer party.

We started that morning with Bloody Marys on the pier, and as the guests arrived, everyone seemed pleased that we had missed another storm. As the day went on, the storm changed from a tropical storm to a category 1 hurricane. We were not watching TV and had the CDs playing on the stereo instead of the radio. At the same time, we had increasing wind speed, and it also took a hard turn to the north. We were completely unaware of these changes as the party went on. By the time the sun went down, we had noticed that the wind was picking up, but nobody really cared. The alcohol had deadened our ability to notice the change in conditions. We just thought that it was windy. The drinks were cold, and the Jimmy

Buffett music on the stereo was loud. The company was friendly. We didn't have any information for anybody to really notice.

Around midnight as twenty of our friends stood on the dock with drinks in their hands, a car pulled up in the driveway. All of a sudden, a million-watt spotlight lit up the entire end of the pier. At first, we thought it was just a latecomer to the party. We all looked directly into the light, trying to hold one another up, laughing and pointing at the bright light. A loudspeaker voice called out, "Ladies and gentlemen, the governor of the state of Alabama has declared this island closed due to Hurricane Juan. You have been asked to evacuate immediately."

"We are too drunk to drive," we yelled back.

"Then we suggest you guys at least get inside before your asses get blown away." We understood that loud and clear and took the party inside the house.

There was no real damage to the house, and nobody was hurt. The Labor Day celebration became a big sleepover for twenty friends.

We threw a party for opening the beach house every year either during the first or second week of May once all the work on the beach property was done. Those were some of the best parties. One year Pat Thompson and I decided to do a pig roast instead of the normal barbecue chicken. This was going to be a real pig roast, not one on the grill. We were going to dig a hole in the sand and cook the pig in the hole the way they did it in Jamaica. Pat and I had taken our wives there, and we figured it looked simple and straightforward enough that even we could do it. Pat purchased the pig from a farmer in north Baldwin County, and we drove over there to pick it up. Pat was an insurance salesman then and drove a nice car that he owned. I was driving a company car then, so we thought my company car would not be a good thing to put a dead pig in, so we used Pat's car. We figured that the lack of a truck was not a problem. We would put the pig in the trunk of Pat's convertible, so off we went to get the pig.

When we got to the farmer's house, the 125 pounds of pig would not fit in the small trunk of the car. After a couple of beers with the farmer standing by, we decided it was not a problem. We would put the pig in the front seat of the car for the trip back across the county and to the beach. So we sat the pig up in the seat. For some reason, Maureen, Pat's wife, had left a wig in the car. We put the wig and a pair of sunglasses on him, and off we drove to the beach house.

Before we started the long trip down Fort Morgan Road, we decided that we needed to get some gas and pulled into the gas station that was at the corner of Fort Morgan and Highway 59. Back in those days, gas stations still had attendants who pumped your gas for you. The attendant was pumping the gas and kept looking over at the pig in the front seat. He would look away, and we would laugh to ourselves. When Pat followed the attendant into the store to pay for the gas, the attendant looked at Pat and said, "I'm sorry to say this, sir, but that is the ugliest woman I've ever seen." Pat and I laughed all the way back to the beach house.

Over the years we have thrown a lot of great parties. My wife, the consummate hostess, threw an annual Christmas party at our house in Fairhope that grew to the point that we were sending out more than 150 invitations for the first Saturday in December every year for many years. The damn party cost an arm and a leg. We had two bars complete with bartenders and two rooms full of food that was manned by two waitresses. It was an open house, which meant that people were supposed to come and go. Our problem was that people came and stayed. The party spilled out into the yard and the porches. Every inch of the house was full of guests.

We finally had to stop most of the parties when my wife ran for public office and won. The list of people we "must invite" became longer than the "want to invite" list. It had gotten to the point that most of the people were business associates and not friends. The party was a lot of work, and we decided that we needed to stop while we were ahead. When we decided not to have the party, it was amazing the number of people who called to ask where their invitations were or to find out if Jackie was upset with them and hadn't invited them.

I'm looking up at the beach house and see someone up there. Well, what have we here? Somebody from the house is finally coming out to see what is up on the end of the pier. I can see into the yard, and it looks like there is a crowd growing in the house. I can't tell who they are or what they are doing, but it must be another celebration of some sort. Damn, I'm getting old and can't remember anything. I recognize the person walking toward the pier without him even looking up at me. It is my son's best friend, Steve Lowell. How strange. I haven't see this kid in years.

Steve is now more than fifty years old. He and my son were best friends from their time in high school. They got in all the normal teenager trouble, wrecking cars, drinking too much, and chasing girls. A young man is like a strong, proud stallion. He runs proud and free and alone. Nothing is so important that it cannot be enjoyed as his wild oats are sown. His dreams are big, his expectations unlimited, and his destiny is in his own hands. The whole world waits to be shown what he can do. My son and Steve were young stallions. They had really become good friends at the University of Alabama, when Danny was a freshman and Steve was hanging out, waiting for somebody to discover that he had stopped going to classes. They had spent spring break together at the beach Danny's junior and senior years in high school. Once they both got out of the university—they may have actually been asked to leave, but we are not sure to this day—they had fumbled around Fairhope for a year, not doing much of anything.

In 1980, my wife and my son started a linen service in Gulf Shores. This was the year after the biggest hurricane to hit Gulf Shores at the time, Hurricane Frederick. This was the hurricane that changed the island community and the lives of all the people living in the area forever. Immediately following Frederick, the condos and hotels had taken over where only single-family homes had been before. What once was a sleepy little coastal community of family homes going back generations and small mom-and-pop businesses had been discovered thanks to the Weather Channel. The hurricane destroyed enough of the island that some families just decided it wasn't worth it to rebuild. Once the money started flowing into the community, it didn't stop. In the days prior to the hurricane, you knew most everyone on the island. After the hurricane the developers took over, and the tourist followed. The developers built the condos, and the tourist brought their money.

With the tourist came the need for all kinds of services. My wife was brilliant enough to recognize the opportunity and opened a linen service with a friend of hers named Arden Ward. These ladies had hired my son as their delivery boy. Once the business took off, Danny had talked us into hiring Steve. The boys had worked in the terrible heat of a Laundromat for twelve-hour days to make sure that the deliveries were on time.

When we first started the business, we couldn't really afford enough inventory of linens, so the boys would pick up the sheets and towels in the morning and run them back to the shop to be washed so that we could return them to the housekeepers in the afternoons before check-ins. They would run in the back door with sheets, towels, and washcloths, and we would wash, dry, and fold them as fast as possible to deliver them back to the hotels and condos before the cleaning staff had finished the rooms and were ready for the new linens. We did all of this while it was 90 degrees outside and 120 inside the linen service. The industrial dryers made it impossible to cool down, so we had industrial fans blowing the hot air around to keep everyone from passing out.

These two boys were in their early twenties and full of piss and vinegar. In addition to all the hotels and condos, they had the bar route where they delivered table linens and bar towels to all the new bars and the old locally owned bars. They were both good-looking kids, tall and blond with good tans, living at the beach and working hard all day and running hard all night. All the ladies who worked at the bars and restaurants loved them. Each day they planned what the night would include before they got off work at five o'clock. I don't think that either of them ever bought a drink for the three years that they worked the bar route. They knew everybody, and everybody knew them.

This was all a long time ago, and this man walking to the end of the pier had grown up and changed a great deal since last I had seen him.

Steve walked out to the end of the pier and immediately went to the ice chest. He reached in and took out a Miller Lite, opened the beer, and, without another word, drank down half. "Ah, coldest beer in town," he said with a chuckle.

It was a joke among the locals that every bar in Gulf Shores and the neighboring city of Orange Beach bragged that they had the coldest beer in town. Steve walked over to the bench, and instead of sitting, he hopped up on the railing and balanced there, sipping the can in his hand.

"You know," he began and seemed to be thinking very hard about what he was saying, "I've spent hours, hell, days on the end of this pier. I've been coming here for more than twenty years."

He looked up at the upper deck of the pier, which we jokingly referred to as the "clothing optional" deck. The upper deck was a ten-by-ten-foot area that has latticework all the way around the sides, making it impossible to see from the house or any other pier. This was specifically done for when we were younger and liked to lie out in the sun without anything on.

"Made out with my wife the first time right up there," he said, pointing to the top deck. Of course, he was not the only kid who had done that. I had heard this tale several times from other friends over the years.

"Danny and I sat here many days, drinking your beer," Steve continued. "The very best thing about this pier was always Dad's ice chest." He laughed. Then he raised his beer in the direction of the ice chest like a toast.

"You know, the best memories I have of us—you, me, and Danny— were all those days at the Pink Pony Pub. Danny and I would work our asses off all weekend long. We'd get everything back together on Monday, and then we would have Tuesdays off to play. I remember you getting off work in the afternoons when you still worked in Fairhope and driving down to meet us at the Pony. Remember buying Danny and me those beer steins? You know the white ones with the Pink Pony logo on them of a horse sitting at the bar? What did they cost back then? Twenty? Twenty-five dollars?" He looked at the deck of the pier. "They were priceless."

Steve looked off into the distance. It had been a long time since those days, but memories that dear aren't easily forgotten. "You had our names put on them, the beer mugs. We thought we were the coolest guys in town. Only the big condo developers had their own Pink Pony mugs back then. We felt like we had really made it big.

"There we were two guys in our twenties with zero extra money. We spent everything we had on the apartment we stayed in. We never realized that by joining the Pony club, we would get the beer half price. You bought both of us one of those mugs, and they hung over the bar between the mayor and a state senator's mug." The rule was once you purchased the mug, you left it at the bar, and it was there for your next visit. "You probably saved us a ton of money on beer." He laughed and continued, "But then Danny had a way of flirting with all the bartenders and getting a lot of beer for free."

He took a long drink from his beer can. "I don't think I ever remembered to tell you thanks for that. It meant more than you know. You were like a dad to me back then. More of a friend than anybody who was much older should have been. There was Jackie working our butts off during the day.

Hell, she worked us harder when we had hangovers just to prove a point. And then you were buying us beer every time you could."

Steve took the last drink of beer from the can. "Coldest beer in town," he said and laughed.

In the house somebody turned on the stereo, and it starting playing Jimmy Buffett on the end of the pier.

"I wonder how many hours of Buffet you have?" He crushed his can and hopped off the railing. He opened Dad's ice chest and got another beer out of the bottom. He turned and started walking back up the pier toward the house.

"Love you, Byron," he said, wiping his hand across his eyes.

As Steve got to the end of the pier where it turned into a grassy yard, his two kids and his wife met him. It is so amazing to see all the kids grown up. Steve is a fine man, a good husband, and a good father. I'd love to think I had something to do with that, but who knows?

One of the things that I was known for in my younger days was my ability to talk to kids about priorities. I had the priority discussion with my kids, your kids, the neighborhood kids, complete stranger's kids. My kids learned very early that when they had done anything wrong, the first question I asked was always going to be "What are your priorities?" They would give me flak about these discussions once they got older, but when they were in trouble and I still had control like in their junior high school years, they knew that the punishment included a priority discussion. The torture was to get them to sit still and verbalize to me why they had done something stupid like wreck their new car while trying to get an older guy named Cono Adkinson to buy them booze before they were old enough to drink. They were smart kids, and we tried to give them the best education we could; however, they needed to understand that education was a wonderful thing and that it might make you look smart but that only the correct application of that education would make you wise. These talks are my own private revenge against my kids for making me crazy. They did some crazy things like all kids do, but the priority discussions were retribution.

I would be sitting quietly either on the pier or the porch, waiting when they got home. My favorite priority discussions came when they had been drinking. There was nothing more fun than having your kids try to have a philosophical discussion with you when they were half lit and trying to hide it from you, faking sobriety.

I am amazed every day that my daughter's eyes still work. That she can even look straight ahead is a miracle. Her favorite response to the priority discussion was to roll her eyes up in her head. I am sure that she could tell you exactly what the inside of her brain looked like because those eyes of hers spent more than half the time rolling around and looking at her skull or at least half the time when she was talking to me.

When Danny wanted to drop out of basketball and take art classes, we talked about priorities. When Donna decided to pass up a scholarship to Birmingham-Southern and follow her brother to the University of Alabama, we discussed priorities. The time Danny said he wanted to sell his motorcycle and buy a convertible Mustang, we discussed priorities. When Donna wanted to skip her senior year of high school and go to college a year early, we discussed priorities. I tried not to force the kids to take my decisions without answering their questions openly and honestly. We always believed that teaching them how to make a decision was more important than telling them what the right decision was. These discussions were the priority discussions. I believe these discussions paid off. Sometimes they worked out to my benefit, and sometimes they didn't.

Both my kids turned out okay, even though one of them only made it to twenty-two years old.

Chapter 12

I'm looking out over the water, and I feel the pier beginning to sway. One of the downsides of a single-piling pier is that it sways when people walk on it. It's good that you have a little warning when people are coming, especially if you are lying in the sun with your eyes closed or you are napping. I turn around to see the six foot six inches of long and tall Alan Bryars walking to the end of the pier.

Alan and I have been friends since the first day I joined Perdido River Hunting Club. He was a happy guy of forty when I met him. He spent his weekdays driving an eighteen-wheeler truck from Bay Minette to Montgomery, Alabama, so he was alone a lot of the time. When he came to the hunting club, he was the center of the conversations. Alan is almost fifteen years younger than I am, but he has always had an old soul. It may have been all the time he spent alone in the truck, listening to world news reports, or it may have been that he was such an avid reader. But when you talked to him, you got the sense that he had been thinking very hard about difficult subjects. He had gone through a terrible midlife crisis in his forties, and he and his wife, Kathy, had not survived it. Alan and I had some heavy conversations during that time, and I tried to get him to work it out with her. We even had a priority discussion sitting by the firepit at the hunting club. A firepit seems to work no matter what age you are. Well, generally, they do.

Alan was one of the first people I met when I joined Perdido River Hunting Club years ago. I was never a hunter until I turned forty and started looking for things to do during the winter when it wasn't beach season. My best friend in life, Mark Cramton, was a member, and he decided that I needed to join the all-guys club. Not being much of a hunter, I preferred taking pictures of the deer, I decided that I would go along and take a camera. I took interesting pictures of deer and shared them with all the serious hunters who seemed to never see a thing. In one of the discussions that Alan and I had by the fire one night, he told me that the other guys were having quite the laugh about me taking pictures and not hunting. I was seeing a lot more deer than they were, but they laughed because I didn't want to shoot the deer.

After Alan got a cold beer and sat down on the top of the five steps that led from the main deck of the pier to the lower deck, which was a boat platform, he gazed out over the water and took a sip of beer. This is a natural reaction to large bodies of water, I think—gazing out. I've seen a hundred people do the same thing. It doesn't really matter what body of water it is either. People just love to stare at water. Alan sat quietly and studied the water.

The pier actually has four different levels. The main deck was on level with the front yard, and when you walk out on the pier, you are on this level. You walk out the one hundred feet runway to the main seating area. This is a twenty-foot-by-twenty-foot deck with a pole in the center of it for support. A table surrounds the pole, and over the years that table has been round, square, and octagon-shaped depending on my wife's opinion at the time. The table changes every time we rebuild the pier, and that seems lately to be every other year because of the storms.

The second level was a fish-cleaning pier, which is four feet lower than the main deck of the pier with a four-foot fishing-cleaning table complete with water. This level is four feet wide but only three feet long, and it ends with steps that go into the water.

The third level was off the front end of the main deck, and it is six feet long and four feet wide. This level has a boat lift on one side and an in-water boat slip on the other side. It was not unusual to have company show up by boat and stay for several days.

The last level was a roof over part of the main deck, and it was eight feet higher than the main deck. It was twenty feet long to cover the whole width of the main deck but only six feet wide, so it allowed people to get sun on the main deck while some people sat in the shade. The roof deck was also referred to as the clothing-optional deck.

Alan sat on the top step of the stairs that went down to the boat level of the pier. The sun is starting to set, and I hope that he stays long enough to watch the pinks and oranges that take over the sky during a sunset. I've watched the sun set over water all over the world from Africa to Key West, Florida, but no other sunset brings the same emotion for me as the ones from the end of this pier. When the sun drops like a big red M&M into the water, you believe that you are at the end of the world and heaven is opening its arms to you. I've watched these color and light shows for fifty years, and I still catch myself holding my breath for those last few seconds, wishing the sky could stay that beautiful all the time.

Alan interrupted my thoughts by asking, "Do you remember that weekend that you came up to Perdido River and we sat by the firepit, talking about what my situation was with my ex-wife?"

Of course I remembered. Alan had lost his father to illness and his wife to divorce. He had taken to calling me Pop even though we were only fifteen years apart. Actually, just about everyone calls me Pop now. He and I sat by the firepit and philosophized about life. I tried to give him my perspective on things, not really advice, just a different look at things that I had figured out over the years. I guess it was just more of the priority talk that I had given the kids. He seemed to listen but still made a lot of the same mistakes that I had made at his age.

The particular discussion that he was thinking of occurred when he and his wife of twenty years had decided to call it quits and get a divorce. I had tried every angle that I could think of to keep him from making what I thought was a mistake. I had used the reasons of the mind—a lost second income, lost houses, lost toys. I had tried the reasons of the heart—a lost love, a lost friendship, a lost partner. Then I had tried the reasons of the soul. "You can't replace the person who knows how to take care of you when you're sick, the person who understands when to ask what's wrong and when to not say a word, the person who knows when you need to hear that it's okay and when you need to hear that you should stop feeling sorry for yourself," I had said. It takes the soul a long time to grow so close to someone that they know all these things about you, and it is very hard to replace that soul mate when you are almost fifty years old and starting over like he had.

Unfortunately, none of my sage advice was taken, and they got the separation and then the divorce. It was a sad time at the hunting camp because everyone loved them both. As I had feared, the divorce changed him. He had gone from a playful, fun-loving married guy to a bitter, sarcastic, pessimistic unmarried guy. Divorce seemed to do that to my friends. They either learned to love deeper and more honestly, or they gave up and began to think that the world had been unfair to them, putting up walls to protect themselves and then wondering why nobody wanted to be around them anymore.

"You were right," Alan whispered, studying the label on the Miller Lite in his hand.

This was not one of those times when I wanted to hear that I was right. I had hoped with each of my friends that they would be able to find the happy medium that my wife and I had found. I knew that we were the exception to the rule, having been together all our lives. I did not want to say I told you so. I wanted him to know that I was still sorry for his pain.

"Alan?" someone called from the front yard. We both turned to see a lovely bleach blonde with long tanned legs and a very short skirt standing in the yard, holding her hand up to her eyes to block the setting sun.

"You ready to go, honey?" she called again without taking a step onto the pier.

I noticed that she has on three-inch spike heel sandals, and I understood. The pier is wood with quarter-inch spaces between the boards. It was not a good thing to try to walk in those shoes in the sand or down the pier. It didn't matter to me what was on the bottom of her feet. It was what she had above those feet that made me smile. She was a looker.

"Thanks, man," Alan said. "I love you, Byron," and with that, Mr. Bryars took a final gulp, brushed something that looked like a tear off his cheek, and walked back up the hundred feet to meet the blonde.

I sigh to no one, knowing that the arm around his waist was not the one he needed. He put his arm around her beautiful tanned shoulders and walked out to his truck.

He would get it right eventually, and I hoped that it would be sooner rather than later. There is nothing that I can do for him at this point. We must all live with our own decisions to the end.

Alan is not the only friend I've watched divorce a good lady. Probably one of the hardest on both Jackie and me was Jim and Margie Life. Jim and

Margie had moved to Fairhope when their kids and ours were in preschool. The Lifes had three kids, and our two fell right in between theirs. Keith was the oldest—two years older than Danny. Jeff was a little younger than Danny and a little older than my daughter. Their youngest was Lyndi, who was two years younger than my daughter.

We meet the Lifes at the Trinity Church one Sunday and made a friendly offer for them to stop by the house sometime. We gave them directions, and that afternoon there was a knock on the door. It was all five of them. We quickly put the kids in the yard to play and sat down to talk. From that day to now, we all have remained close. Even though Jim and Margie have been divorced and remarried to other people, we all stayed in touch over these fifty years. Jim moved his family to Arkansas and raised his kids to be fine adults. All of them are successful, kind, humble, fun-loving people. They are all very different and creative. The different part comes from Jim. He cut his own path in life. Margie was the creative one. She has an eye for design, color, art, and elegances. We traveled with Jim and Margie while they were together and also after the divorce with Jim and Margie separately. They never made us feel bad or forced us to choose between them. It was true friends who can share you with someone else and not ask for your full commitment to them alone.

Before I came out on this pier—yesterday or the day before, I don't really remember—Jim was the last person I spoke to on the phone. I'm not sure what I said, and I don't remember what he said. But with us it wasn't about what we said. It was just that we were always there in the best and worst of times for each other. Shortly after my son died, Jim was having an issue with one of his boys. I don't even remember what the argument was about, but Jim was telling me that he hadn't spoken to his son in more than a week because of the disagreement. I was bullshit mad. I told him that I had just lost my son and that I'd do anything in this world to have one more conversation with him, and here he was not talking to his son because of some stupid disagreement. That was probably the maddest I've ever been at Jim Life. Of course, I know now that it wasn't really Jim that I was upset with. It was the loss of my son. Jim was a brilliant man. He knew what my problem was, but he did get on the phone and patch up the relationship, probably just to shut me up.

Jim and I spent days just sitting on the end of this pier. We solved many problems over this body of water. We talked through decisions about wives, kids, business, and priorities. When we both retired, Jim would come down to the beach house, and mostly, it was just me and him for a week. We might do a little fishing, but we usually sat and talked. One time Jim was here, and we were throwing our cast nets out in front of the pier. Jim was on one side of the pier, and I was on the other with the bucket. We had a few fish in the bucket already, and all of a sudden, Jim saw a puffer fish in his net. This was unusual as we don't get many puffer fish in the nets or around the pier. Jim helped the little thing get out of the net, but then the puffer fish ran up the leg of his swim shorts. Jim was hopping around, trying to push the fish back down the leg of his shorts, but the more he moved, the bigger the fish blew up. The more the fish puffed up, the more Jim jumped around and scared the little fish. I was no help. All I could do was laugh and fall over in the water. We finally got the fish loose, and he swam away; however, it was a close call there for a few minutes. I wasn't sure who to save—the fish or the man.

When the kids were preteenagers, Jackie and I drove all the way to Indiana to visit the Lifes. Jim had taken a job there, and we had never been, so off we went in our blue station wagon. Jim and Margie had driven to see us in Tennessee when we lived up there for a short time. We had taken trips to New Orleans with Jim and Margie without the kids. And when Jim had settled in Arkansas, we had taken a trip to visit them in their new house. It seems that no matter where we have lived, the two of our families have always been connected. The kids still stay in touch. Even when Keith was living in England, he came back to visit and went with us to the hunting camp for the weekend. Friends like these are better than anything else in life. They are better than fame or fortune. They make you feel warm and loved with just a short phone call or a picture calendar like Jim made for years.

The sun is setting over Mobile Bay, and the clouds tonight are not the fluffy, big, and fat kind. Instead they are the long, flat ones that stretch for a mile or two like someone took the fluffy versions and rolled over them with a rolling pin from heaven, flattening them out. The sun is still falling into the water, and then it peeks out of the bottom side of the clouds again after hiding its bright red face. It's like a boy hiding his face behind a pillow because he doesn't want to go to bed.

As the sun drops closer to the water, the skyline goes pink to red with deepening, dark shadows. The water turns darker, and the seagulls seem to know that it will be a colorful show this evening. So the gulls take a seat on the pilings where piers used to be or on the end my neighbor's pier just to watch the explosion of color that is coming within minutes. The sun drops again behind another flat cloud, and instantly, the color beneath the cloud turns the color of an orange and cranberry juice cocktail. All we need is a shot of vodka, and God and all his angels could drink the sky with a straw. The sunset once again peeks its bashful face out from under the cloud, and now with full force, it lights up the sky and the water. It seems that the sunset is always the most amazing right before it hits the water.

It was a wonderful thing to watch, and it does not matter how many times I have seen the sun set over our Mobile Bay. Our sunsets always make everyone leave the house and walk to the end of the pier for a full view of the vibrant, multicolored show. If you believe that this life is all there is and there is no greater power than man, you must walk to the end of this pier at sunset. If you watch the sky above turn baby blue and horizon turn pink, red, and purple, you will never doubt the existence of God again. Never.

I sit on the pier, looking due west into the expanse of Mobile Bay. I know that I am not a traditional religious man. I haven't been for many years, but something bigger than anything on this earth is responsible for this stunning daily event.

As the sun finally drops an inch at a time into the water, I feel the temperature drop a few degrees with each inch it fades. Movement catches my eye, and a young women three piers down walks to the end of the other pier. It's the Nelsons' pier, but I'm not sure who this young woman is. She holds a camera in her hand. I think to myself, *Go ahead and take all the pictures you want.* Heaven knows over the years we have had many a camera out here. We have tried to capture the color, the emotion, the nightly ballet of birds, and the sun. There is no way. Cameras just are not that good. They cannot capture the true majesty of these moments. It was in the last moment of the sunset that you believe in truth and love, in honesty and friendship, in family and in the southern way of life. No, there is no way to capture the sunsets over Mobile Bay with a camera. You must live them. And no matter how many you may be lucky enough to see in your lifetime, you will never have enough of them. You will always want to see one more. I know that now. I want to see just one more.

Chapter 13

I know that I may sound like I think I am a wise old sage at this point, but I'm not. I don't intend to mislead you. That's not my nature or my intention. I was a crazy young redneck just like the rest of my friends. My wife and I grew up quick, getting married so young and having kids shortly thereafter. But I had my moments when, even though I was a father of two, a faithful husband, and a man trying to get ahead in the business world, I went a little bit off center.

One of these times when I was not so responsible was the motorcycle ride through Fairhope—totally nude. The University of Alabama and Paul "Bear" Bryant were actually responsible for the now famous motorcycle ride. I was still a young man in my early thirties, and we had lived in Fairhope for several years. It was not the upper-class community it is today. Back then it was the eastern shore of Mobile Bay, where trailers sat on waterfront lots. Today it is the Eastern Shore of Mobile Bay, where the trailers have been replaced with four-thousand-square-foot houses with wrapping front porches, white picket fences, and BMWs in the garages. Most of the people are not from Fairhope at all. They've bought their way into our community.

When we first moved to Fairhope, if we wanted a good hamburger, we could find it on our side of the bay at the Jack Ellis on Fairhope Avenue. If we wanted a good steak, we had to go to Mobile. Fairhope had three stoplights on the main street, which was Fairhope Avenue. It was a small town then with no real claim to fame other than it was the only place on earth other than Africa where a jubilee happened.

A jubilee is a freak of nature that occurs when the oxygen level in the water gets very low and the confused marine life rushes to the sandy shore to get out of the water. This allows all the locals to rush to the water's edge and easily pick up all the fish and crabs that they can carry. With the jubilees, your phone would ring in the middle of the night, scaring you half to death. You'd pick up the phone and someone would scream, "Jubilee! At Orange Street pier!"

I would shake my wife awake. Then she would grab my daughter, and I'd grab my son. We threw both sleeping kids in the back of the car, and off we would go to the eastern shoreline of Mobile Bay with flashlights and buckets. The marine life—crabs, mullet, flounders, everything—would be lying on the beach, and all we had to do was walk along and pick them up. It was as simple as picking blackberries off the side of a dirt road. We would fill up our freezer and our neighbor's freezers with so much seafood that we could eat for months.

But let's back to the motorcycle ride. As is normal for a Saturday in the southern part of United States, we had a group of friends over for the Alabama football game. We had been watching the biggest event of the year in the state of Alabama—the Alabama v. Auburn football game, which was known as the Iron Bowl! In Alabama, you are born either an Alabama fan or an Auburn fan. To say that football was important in Alabama is an understatement. Football isn't a big thing. It is the *only* thing! Marriages and families have broken up over the annual game. And a couple of years ago, one lady in Birmingham shot another lady just for saying something about her team. Who wins that one game every year is more important than who wins the governor's race and probably the presidency. Ask people from Alabama what year George Wallace was shot, and maybe one in fifty people can tell you. Ask people from Alabama what year Bear Bryant passed away, and nine out of ten people older than forty will get it right. To this day, the trustee for the University of Alabama will fire a man who wins every game during the year but loses the Auburn game.

The big game is always on the weekend after Thanksgiving and is always another excuse for a tailgate party at the Calhoun house.

This game started out like many others. The men would show up early. We needed to slay the fatted calf. Generally, this was actually chickens. We couldn't afford a fatted calf and probably wouldn't know where to get one anyway. We would cut the chickens into quarters and drink a beer. Then we would build a fire in the grill outside and drink another beer. Somebody would start telling Auburn jokes then. If we were unfortunate enough to have some of those Auburn fans over for the game, they might tell a few Alabama jokes, and we would drink more beers. About a half hour before the game, the women would show up, and by then the men were about half in the bag. We would need one of them to make a beer run by that time because we were all too drunk to get it on our own. We were so happy when the kids got old enough to drive because back then when they knew you at the store, they would let your kids pick up the beer if you called ahead.

It was a fact of life with the Alabama v. Auburn game that once the final whistle was blown and the final score was posted, the losing team will without provocation make a bet on next year's game. Before the recruiting has begun and before the dust has settled on the current year, the fans of Alabama and Auburn will make wagers about the next football game, which is 364 days away. It was this type of discussion at the Elks Lodge in Fairhope during the year before when a lowlife Auburn friend came up with the idea for the motorcycle ride.

I don't remember who or what started the discussion, which quickly turned into a football argument. I was sitting with an Auburn fan named Duck Gunnison, who was a good friend other than his lack of taste in Alabama football teams. Then he said he was sure that there was no way in hell that Alabama would beat Auburn this year. Now, it was the early summer, and little was known about either team; however, with enough cold beer, I will take just about any bet. So without knowing what the bet was, I said with all the conviction that a true fan could muster, "I'll take that bet." As the lowlife Auburn enthusiast, Duck said, "Okay, you dumb-ass. Whoever loses has to streak through Fairhope buckass naked immediately following the game." It was the early '70s, and streaking was a national pastime. Again, with more Miller Lite speaking than me speaking, I quickly added, "You'd better lose some weight, fat boy, because you naked downtown is not a Kodak moment."

You would think that as months passed, Duck and I would have forgotten about the bet and moved on to other things. The amount of beer consumed should have erased the bet from our minds. Unfortunately for me, it didn't. The game day came, and Duck and his wife, Marlene, came to watch the game at my house with all our Alabama friends. We must have had thirty-five people, not counting kids, for the game. The University of Alabama was considerable behind by halftime. It was the kickoff for the second half when Duck decided to remind me about the bet that we had made the previous spring. I wondered that if Auburn had not had such a big lead if Duck's memory would have been so clear. I doubt it.

As the game progressed, the day became more ominous as the points kept being added to the wrong side of the scoreboard. With the final play, the Alabama fans were all on their feet, screaming at the television as if the players could hear us up in Tuscaloosa. With the final play came an Alabama fumble, and a hush fell over the room. Thirty-four pairs of eyes fell on me. Duck, being totally confident in his team, had taken a seat in my easy chair for the whole fourth quarter, not saying a word. I turned to look at him, and the grin on his face was sinister. "Checkmate!" he said.

Now a man who does not have a lot must have at least one thing always, and that is his word. Without your word, you have no integrity, and without integrity, you have no honor. Without honor, you are no better than a kudzu vine. Kudzu is the most useless and annoying of all things in the state of Alabama. I could not be useless and annoying. I had only one choice, and that was to pay off the bet. And so I looked Duck Gunnison in his red face, called him a son of a bitch, and opened another beer. I stood at the ice chest and drank it all the way down in one long gulp. I thought for a minute, hands on my hips, staring at Duck and the rest of my friends who stood by smiling at me. Then I went over to my motorcycle, a recent purchase, and threw my leg over the seat, cranking it up. When I pulled out of the driveway, everyone was frozen in place. A chorus of voices rang out. "No way!" "What? Is he kidding?" "My God, he has lost his mind." The last comment about my sanity came from my wife, and the comment followed me up the street toward downtown Fairhope.

For a solid minute, my friends and Duck stood in stunned silence. Then total chaos broke out as everyone ran for their cars to follow behind the fool on the Honda 250. I had a good two-minute head start on them, but they all knew the best place to start the ride. Everyone knew that if I was really going to do this thing, they knew where I would start out.

Now let me clarify a few details for you if you're not from Fairhope. The road through the middle of town is called Fairhope Avenue. It is usually the busiest road in the town, and it was Saturday. The good news was that it was the equivalent of Super Bowl Sunday in Alabama, so most people were at home or at a bar in front of the television still. So my timing was actually good for the situation. Fairhope Avenue runs from east to west through the middle of town. There were stoplights back then, one in the intersection of Fairhope and Section and the other one block east at the corner of Fairhope and Belange. Fairhope Avenue ended at what the locals call the Big Pier. It was then a three-hundred-yard-long pier with a circle turnaround for the parking lot. The Big Pier sat at the bottom of a large red clay bluff, which made for a steep hill going down to or coming up from the bay. I drove down to the bottom of the hill and stopped the Honda to think. It only took a minute to figure out. If I was going to do this, I needed to get moving and quick. I stripped off my shirt and then my jeans. Lastly, I took off my BVDs and stuffed everything into the backpack on the rear of the bike. I wasn't even wearing a pair of sunglasses, but I did put my socks and boots back on for safety.

Did I mention it was November? And as I remember it now, it was very cold. *No time like the present*, I thought, and then I took off up the hill and through the middle of town. I was doing fine until I saw that my friends, about fifteen carloads of people, were all lined up at the stoplight at the corner of Fairhope and Section Street. They were laughing and clapping and cheering. I drove right through the middle of them, grinning and naked as the day I was born, at about twenty miles per hour. And then two things happened to wipe that grin off my face.

I mentioned that it was a slow day in downtown Fairhope because of the game. It was also a slow day for the Fairhope Police Department. There were only two police cars out that day, and noticing the caravan of cars headed for downtown Fairhope, they had followed. When I came up the hill, one of the police cars got behind me. The other coming the opposite way saw a naked man on a motorcycle and quickly stopped his car in the middle of the road under the stoplight. The one behind me turned on his lights and siren, but I wasn't stopping. I ran through the red light and kept going to the house.

As it turned out, the officer behind me had picked me up at the top of the hill and followed me all the way through town when we finally got back to my house and had a chance to talk to him. He said he noticed two things. The first was that I was naked. The second was that I was Byron Calhoun. I had lived here for many years, and I knew all the police officers because it was a really small town back then. In fact, we all belonged to the Elks Lodge. I saw these guys every Friday night, and they knew what I drove. The one behind me was Ronnie, a friend whose son I coached in Little League softball. The one in front of me was Bill, a friend of the family. I had known Bill for fifteen years. Bill had no idea it was me. I was traveling pretty fast by the time I passed him at the stoplight. He jumped out of his police car and drew his weapon, standing in a shooting stance with the gun pointed at my bare chest. About that time Ronnie screamed over the radio, "Don't shoot, Bill! It's Byron!" At the last minute, he lowered his gun, and I kept going through the stoplight and around his car, headed for home.

A few days later after a long day at work, I was sitting at the Elks Lodge when Bill walked in. He was not in uniform. He was in his regular street clothes. He walked slowly up to the bar and sat on the stool next to mine. Everybody had heard the story, and everyone in the place stopped to watch what was going to happen. The place was dead silent. I ordered him a beer, his favorite brand, even though it was a little more expensive, and he whispered a thank-you. We sat in silence for several minutes while Bill finished his beer. Nobody said a word, but all eyes were on us.

Bill did not hurry through his beer. I did not say a word. I just continued to drink my Miller really slowly. Bill finished his beer and waved a thank-you to the bartender. As he turned to go, he pulled a sheet of paper from the pants pocket of his jeans. He tossed the paper on the bar in front of me, slapped me on the back, and walked directly out the door.

Nobody moved. Nobody said a word. I drank down the last of my beer and put the glass down on the paper napkin on the bar. I took another napkin and wiped my hand so I didn't get water on the paper that Bill had left. I opened the white sheet of paper and read the few lines. I quietly refolded the paper and put it into my shirt pocket. I picked up the fresh beer that the bartender put down and took another drink. That was all the peanut gallery could take. All at once five guys were grabbing at my shirt pocket to get to the sheet of paper that the police officer had given me. It was Mark Cramton who got it out of my pocket and read it with two other guys looking over his shoulder.

"It's a ticket," he said and laughed with tears in his eyes. "It's a fine of fifteen dollars for running a red light."

It took several years to get even with Duck Gunnison, but Mark and I were able to do it. Duck, Mark, and I all decided to take the wives on a long weekend to South Florida. We loaded up the cars and made the eight-hour trip to the west coast of Florida, leaving the kids and our cares behind. Duck had long forgotten about the lost bet, and his guard was down. We had a great time Friday and Saturday.

The Florida lottery is played twice a week, on Wednesday and Saturday. That Sunday morning our dearest friend Bruce Childress came up with a way to get back at Gunnison. Mark and I went to the convenience store at the end of the block and bought the Sunday-morning paper. The lottery numbers were posted in the paper, and we quickly looked up the winning numbers from the night before. We then purchased a ticket for the next drawing using the winning numbers from the night before.

When we got back to the condominium that we had rented for the weekend, we causally threw the lottery tickets and the newspaper on the table. Then we waited. Duck got up, and while he was having his morning coffee, he asked whose lottery tickets those were on the table. "Marlene's," we all said. Marlene was his wife, and she was in on the trick. Duck looked up the winning lottery numbers and knew that the ticket was a winner. He never looked at the date on the tickets.

Duck wet wild, hugging his wife and screaming that he was rich. He had won almost $10 million. We all played along. We went to dinner that night, and Duck picked up the check. After all, he was rich. On the way home on Monday, Duck thought it would be a great idea for everyone to stop in Tallahassee and go to the lottery office to pick up his winnings. It was at that point that we decided to point out that the date was wrong.

Gunnison did not speak to any of us for the next eight hours while we drove home.

Roll Tide!

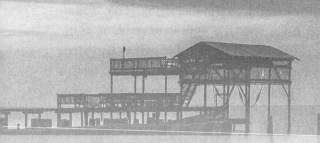

CHAPTER 14

There are people up at the house. Two people walk out of the screened-in porch and down the steps to the yard.

My eyesight has not been the best since I was in my twenties, but in my fifties, my eyesight had gone to hell. But my vision is the least of my concerns. The winter before my fiftieth birthday, I had my first major heart attack and a triple bypass. They told us at the time that the work they did would last ten years, and then something else would probably need to be done. The doctors at that time were very excited about the progress that was being made with bypass surgery, and they believed that in ten years when I was due for another plumbing procedure, their methods would be light-years ahead of where they were then. My second and third heart attacks, which happened in my sixties, were less severe but just as scary. By that time, I knew the early signs and got to the hospital, which was only minutes away from our house in Fairhope. The doctors were right. The procedures had improved, but in my case, they had not improved enough. The damage done to my heart could never be fixed, but I'm getting ahead of myself.

Once the two figures get to the end of the yard and begin walking down the pier, they're close enough to see. I can tell that it is Pat and Peter. These are two of my very dearest friends. I had known Patricia or Pat for forty years, and I had known Peter, her husband, for fifteen.

I met Pat Miller when she was just barely out of high school. She had come to work for the printing company in Fairhope, Poser Business Forms.

It was a large printing company, and I was the supervisor when Pat started working there. I was the district operations manager over four states when I quit after twenty years. It was a great job, but the travel at the end was too much for my family. I missed a lot of things with my kids and spent time on weekends building the beach house.

I had met Pat Miller through Poser's, and she and my wife had become best friends over the years. I wonder as Pat and Peter walk to the end of the pier what they are doing down here tonight. I can see several shadows in the house, so maybe Jackie just hasn't made it out here yet.

Pat worked for me in customer service when I was in charge of the plant in Fairhope. She was a natural salesperson and customer-focus person. She has worked for Poser's through several changes in management and ownership over the years. She left for a short time when she married Peter. He had also worked for the printing company when it was purchased by Print Excel. Peter had been a corporate compliance guy from headquarters, and when he was sent to Fairhope from Colorado, he fell hard and fast for that petite and crazy Alabama girl. Pat is outspoken, funny, smart, and lovable. She does not pull a punch when it comes to her opinion. She was a bit of a party girl when she was younger, but after she married Peter, she calmed down.

I remember one weekend when Pat was still single, she had come down to the beach house with a broken heart and a chip on her shoulder that only cold beer and sunshine would take care of. She and I had made a pact to see how much beer two people could drink between sundown Friday and sundown on Sunday. We started on Friday evening, and by Sunday we had consumed seventy-five beers between the two of us. We drank, and then we took naps. Whatever time it was when we got up, we drank again. Pat weighs 115 pounds soaking wet, but she held her own with me. We sat on this pier, and we talked for hours until the hours turned into days and then a whole weekend. My wife and our friend Anna just sat back, watching and laughing at us. We talked about the loves she had known—the good ones who had gotten away and the bad ones she had thrown away. We talked about our kids and her grandkids. She talked a little about work. She knew that I was always interested in what went on at Poser's, even though I had left by this time. But Pat is not the kind of person who likes talking about her job anyway. She is the best that they have, but she never brags about what she does. It was always just a job to her, a means to an end. Twenty years at the same company, and it was always just a job, never a career, and certainly never the definition of who she was. I love that about Pat, that ability to be herself and not be her résumé.

One of the darkest times that Pat and I experienced at Poser's would become known as the Halloween Massacre. The Halloween Massacre was a war between me as management and the union that was trying to get into the company. It was the mid-1970s, and the unions in the South were losing power. The union had attempted to get into our shop, and I had successfully kept them out a couple of times. The last organized push by the union resulted in a vote by the employees. As plant manager at the time, the corporate guys were very honest about the effect that a union would have on their plans for the company. They let me know that a union would result in less jobs and that I would need to clean up the mess afterward if the union got in. The union had scheduled the vote for October 30, and I was at the plant day and night to talk with every employee until I knew that I had done everything possible to keep the union out. These were not just my employees. These people were my friends. I coached their kids in Little League. Many of them went to Trinity Church with my wife and kids. I had been to their weddings and some of the weddings of their kids. This was a threat to the company, but it was a personal one to me.

The fight took months between the union and the company. It had gotten dirty, and it had gotten personal. My wife was getting anonymous threatening phone calls at home, and my children were getting hassled at school. The kids were still in middle school. My son was in sixth grade, and my daughter was in fifth. They were too young to be in the middle of a fight with a major union and a large corporation. I was scared. Those were the days when union fights still got nasty and people got hurt. I restricted my kids from answering the phone and sent them out of town on a vacation for the last couple of days before the vote. We did not go out to dinner in public for a month before the vote. I was getting death threats, and we had to call for police protection against the protestors at the plant.

On October 31, Halloween Day, they finally voted.

On the day of the vote, I had a really bad feeling that it was not going our way and that the union had the necessary votes to get inside our company. I promised that if it came out in our favor, I would do whatever it took to never let this happen again. When the votes were all counted, the company won by three votes. I personally walked around and thanked each employee for giving me the chance to make it work without a union. I felt personally responsible to make it right with all the employees and not let the troublemakers take control of us and cause a long-term problem. I knew that the responsibility to fix this was mine, but I needed to make changes to do it.

The celebration started the minute the plant opened. We had a morning meeting, and again, I thanked each employee for trusting me and what they had done to keep the union out of our shop. My next step was to attack. I called each employee involved in the organizing campaign and fired them on the spot. There were thirty people terminated that day. It felt good but only for a minute. The hundreds of employees who were left were thankful that the bastards were gone, but the union representative had no intention of letting it go. The threats to my family continued for several weeks and then stopped suddenly. I have never been so afraid for my kids and wife before or after that time. If that would have happened today, I would have been in court over retaliation claims, but this was before the damn Democrats had forced through so many laws that tied the hands of managers for making profitable companies.

My daughter later became a human resources manager, and she has never understood the hatred I have for unions. I remember one job she had working in HR for a union shop, and they were trying a new strategy for collaborative negotiations. She was young and new to business and excited about the whole process. She thought that she was blazing new ground that would change the whole adversarial relationship between management and unions into a positive working partnership. Within two months, I got a phone call one night that she was being escorted into the ship building company where she worked by armed guards. The negotiations had fallen apart, and she was getting a bad taste about the battles between management and unions.

Peter and Pat made it to the end of the pier, and without a second thought, Peter went to Dad's ice chest and pulled out two Miller Lites. He opened one for Pat, passing it over to her, and she took a seat. Opening his own, he sat next to her and put an arm around her shoulders.

As they looked across the water, Peter said, "Do you remember the first time I came here?"

Pat laughed.

"I was still living in Colorado and knew nothing at all about Alabama, the beach, or fishing," he said.

Peter was a city boy back then. When he had first come to the beach house, we all thought that Pat had lost her mind. Pat was an outdoorsy kind of girl, not a tomboy but certainly not a girly girl. She loved working in her gardens outside and loved the beach. She had spent lots of time at the beach and had friends who were boat captains and friends who were beach bums with lots of money. Without a doubt, Peter was a training opportunity for her. He knew nothing of the water or the seafood in it. He had never been fishing and certainly never done our kind of fishing.

In Fort Morgan, Alabama, we can still legally use gill nets to catch fish. These are 100- to 150-foot nets that you put out in the water and leave for hours, just hoping that some good things like flounder or mullet will run into the net and you'll have dinner. We were always very successful with these nets, and therein lies the reason that they have been outlawed on most parts of the Gulf of Mexico coastline.

"What's the process for gillnetting, Peter?" Pat asked with a laugh like it was a quiz.

"Step one, you pull the heavy-ass net one hundred feet straight out from the end of the pier," he said very seriously. "Step two, you get back on the pier and open a cold beer. Step three, you drink a second cold beer. Step four, you get back out in the water and run the net by pulling up on the bottom of the net, which creates a hammock where the fish that were innocently swimming along are caught in the net."

I smiled. The student had become a master.

To make this a little harder, you have a large washtub bucket with a rope through the handle tied to your waist. This was just like the flounder days—same bucket, same procedure. As you take the trapped fish out of the net, you throw them in the bucket, screaming like a twelve-year-old girl that you are the master fisherman.

"Step five, walk all the way back to the pier from the end of the net, calling out to whomever was too chicken to get in the water with you that they are a chicken," Peter continued. Generally, he was calling Pat too chicken because she was usually lying in the sun and didn't care about running to the net to get the fish out.

"Step six, get back up on the pier, brag to everyone what a master fisherman you are, open another beer, and repeat the process at step two," Pat finished for him.

Peter calls this redneck fishing, and he may be right. I have watched him learn how to take a catfish out of the net without getting stuck in the finger with one of their stingers. Peter was not the first or the last person to learn about redneck fishing.

The first student of mine was Anna Etheridge. She loved this type of fishing as much as I did. She would stay up all night running the net and sleep on the end of the pier just to see what treasures were in that net. She loved everything about the beach house—fishing, crabbing, finding shells, watching the squirrels, killing snakes, everything.

After I had Anna fully trained on gillnetting, she became the instructor for others. There were many levels to gillnetting. The first level was regular daily fishing with the net. The second level of training in Anna's program was night fishing. This took a little more training, and we would generally get more and different fish in the net at night. The reason night fishing was harder was because you had to hold a light while you tried to get a catfish out of the net without getting stuck in the finger, which would hurt like a son of a bitch!

The third level was cleaning fish that you got out of the net. This was an advanced certification level, and not everyone completed this class successfully. Cleaning fish is an art, not a science, and not everyone is an artist. The top level of gillnetting was mastering the skill of getting a shark out of the net. These were generally baby sand sharks, but they were still a pain in the ass because getting them out of the net while they were still alive and splashing around without getting bitten was a skill. Plus, it was just plain scary after seeing the movie *Jaws*. We even put together the certificate program that Anna facilitated for Peter after his first year at the beach and another friend named Jeff. She led the program over the course of several weekends until they had completed her program. She was so proud when they graduated.

It was Anna who taught them to take the catfish out of the net without getting stuck. Nothing hurts for days like a catfish stick. I have watched Peter stay up all night on the end of the pier with Anna just because the specks and mullet were running. I laughed at him while he learned how to clean a fish. He would make a mess out of the fish and only get small chucks out of the fish. I don't want to make light of it because cleaning a fish is not as easy a skill as one might think. Especially for someone who didn't grow up around it. Peter had progressed a long way toward becoming an Alabama redneck. Pat has loved him through it all.

Pat held on to Peter's hand. "You learned a lot from Byron about fishing and cleaning fish. We owe Bryon a lot."

"I don't know if we would have made it without Byron and Jackie's help," Peter said. "They took us in like their own family, and thank God for that."

Pat laughed. "Hell, I probably would have killed you by now if it wasn't for them."

She gave him a kiss that was as sweet as I'd ever seen.

"And I never trusted him with my dog," Pat said.

Pat had a strict diet for her dog, PJ, when he was a puppy. The dog was a white poodle, and Pat was determined that he was going to be disciplined. Begging and people food were not allowed. I felt sorry for the poor thing and would sneak him little morsels until Pat would catch me and yell at us. One day Pat made the mistake of leaving me with PJ while she ran to the store in Gulf Shores. When she got back, she walked to the end of the pier where PJ and I were sitting. Neither of us moved or said a word.

"Did you give PJ any people food, Byron?" she asked with her hands on her hips. Anna and Jackie were behind her, grinning.

"Nope. I most certainly did not give the dog any people food," I said.

"Then why is PJ orange!" she asked.

PJ had indeed been eating Cheetos with me while they had gone to the store, and his normal white face was covered in orange Cheetos coloring. That just caused her to watch me closer, and I don't know that she ever left me alone with the dog again.

Peter laid his head on Pat's shoulder. Pat held him as tight as she could. Holding on to him was keeping her held together. Peter dropped his head down into her lap and lay there like a child while she played with the hair on the back of his head with her fingers.

"Hey, are we interrupting here?" said Bruce Childress as they walked down the pier.

Peter and Pat stood up to hug two of my favorite people, Bruce and Jane Childress.

"What are you guys up to?" asked Jane.

"Telling Byron stories," said Peter, getting a beer out of the ice chest for Pat.

"There are a lot of those," said Bruce, laughing.

"Remember the trip to Key West?" said Jane with a smile.

Several years ago Jackie and I had gone to Key West with Duck and Marlene Gunnison, Bruce, and Jane. Bruce had a motor home that we always traveled in. We have traveled the country from one side to the other in that motor home. It had everything we needed and gave us so much more freedom to do what we wanted than staying in hotel rooms. Bruce had taught us how to drive the motor home and how to manage life for several weeks living in one. On the trip that Jane was talking about, we had added Duck and Marlene. We had pulled into Boyd's RV campground, parked the motor home, and hooked up everything. We had a couple of drinks sitting outside and then decided to go get dinner.

On this trip we had not taken our tow car, so we unhooked the hoses and took the motor home to dinner. When we got back, Duck had volunteered to hook us back up. A few hours later when had all settled in for the night and were half asleep, there was a loud banging on the door of the motor home. The guys grabbed their jeans and shoes and quickly answered the door. Some strange guy was at the door and yelling, "You have hooked up your rig to my water hose!" When Duck and I tried to get the thing unattached, we realized that Duck had used all his might to tighten it down and we couldn't get it off. We couldn't get it loose. Meanwhile, the crazy guy was yelling about the rules of the campground. As he continued to yell at us, Bruce tried to unhook the hose. The damn thing would not move. As the strange man continued to yell, Duck took his hunting knife out and whacked off the hose. Duck handed the hose to the guy while he stared first at Duck and then at the hose in his hand.

"Let's go, Pete," Pat said after several more minutes. "Jackie needs us now."

The man who had run a multimillion-dollar business pulled himself together and stood straight as a board. He visibly squared his shoulders and reached out his hand for the love of his life, pulling her to her feet.

They stood there for a minute, holding each other with love and support. They turned and walked back toward the house slowly, his arm around her shoulders, her arm around his waist, watching where they stepped.

I turned away from them. It was such a private moment that I had shared with them. I had loved them separately, but I must admit that I loved them more together.

Bruce and Jane watched them go. Bruce reached out for Jane's hand.

"Remember when we rented that boat with Byron and Jackie in Key Marathon?" Bruce asked.

"Yes, of course," Jane answered. "We had been cruising around, sightseeing, and you men decided to stop at that floating swim pier. We all got out of the boat and walked around, looking over the side at the water, looking for fish and crabs."

"We were all standing on the pier, laughing and talking when a guy came up in his boat," Bruce added. "He was hot. Pissed that we were on his private pier."

"Thank goodness that Byron was there," Jane said. "He started talking up the guy, telling him what a great job he had done on the swimming pier."

"He was asking all those questions about how he built his pier and telling him the problems he had with building this pier." Bruce laughed. "The guy ended up telling us that we could stay as long as we wanted."

"Byron knew how to get through to people, didn't he?" Jane said.

We had many great trips with Bruce and Jane. Once we had joined them in Yellowstone, Bruce had driven the motor home, and we flew into West Yellowstone to meet them. We then continued on in the motor home to see Old Faithful, mud plops, painted cliffs, and lots of wild animals. We were driving along and saw some bison. I got out of the motor home and walked up to the bison to take some pictures. Everybody was scared that the bison were going to stampede. A little while later we were watching a herd of elk during their rutting season. I got out to take some pictures, and I guess I got a little too close to the older bull. He started chasing one of the younger bulls away from a female when I got in between them. The older bull was heading straight for me. We all ran for the RV and almost ran over the elks getting away.

"Remember the trip to Alaska with Byron and Jackie?" Jane asked.

"They almost won the ice lottery that time," Bruce said.

Jackie and I had flown to Fairbanks, and Bruce had driven the motor home. We all met up and continued to Anchorage with them. It was always fun. We would hit as many of the tourist spots as possible. He went to the famous Malamute Saloon and saw tons of animals. But the high point of the trip was the clock tower that was built on ice in Nenana River. The Alaskans attached the clock tower by rope to the riverbank. All year long they sell lottery tickets to estimate the date and time when the ice will break and pull the clock tower down, which stops the clock. We all had lottery tickets.

"Byron and Jackie's ticket missed the time by only seven days!" Bruce added.

"We celebrated their fifty-third wedding anniversary near the Arctic Circle with balloons and champagne!" Jane remembered.

They both sat in silence for a minute. Then Bruce added, "We have to carry our fun with us on every trip. Byron and Jackie always brought sacks full every time. Man, what a ride we've all had!"

Jane laughed at Bruce and then hugged him hard.

In my opinion, these two people are two of the finest people on earth. Bruce is a self-made man in the truest sense of the word. They created an extremely successful business for their family that continues to grow now that it is in the hands of their kids. They are kind and generous people. They are two of the most humble and selfless people we have ever known. Jane is perhaps the classiest lady I know but also one of the most creative and fun at the same time.

CHAPTER 15

The sun is up today, and it is another beautiful day at the beach. The sky is blue with streaks of white clouds running through it. The sun is out, but it is not too hot yet. It's June 2 in the Deep South, so it is still bearable. It's not until August that you feel like you're being waterboarded with hot water by Mother Nature.

The footsteps on the pier make me look up, and I see two things I love. One is my daughter, and she is carrying the other, an eighteen pack of Miller Lite. Good thing she has more with all these people coming out here and drinking my cold beer. I've taught the child well. She has in her other hand a bag of ice. She walks over and puts the beer in Dad's ice chest.

She is grown now, and I can't for the life of me remember when that happened. It seems it was only a minute ago that she was six years old. It was her birthday, and we were opening her presents on the tailgate of a truck where the driveway is now. That birthday she got a silver brush and mirror set from her grandmother, Merle. You would have thought she was the princess of the world the way she stared at her reflection and brushed her hair for the rest of the day. She was only six then, but her hair was white blonde until she was in junior high. Now if you look real close, you'll see she is gray at the temples, but she covers it up most of the time. We did all the normal father-daughter things when she was growing up. She had been a Brownie and a Girl Scout, so every year we went to the father-daughter banquet. I would dress up in my very best suit, and her mother had put her in so much crinoline and lace that she made a swishing sound when she walked.

We paid for her to go to White Gloves and Party Manners when she was eight. This was a class for little girls to learn which fork to use and how to sit still, how to say, "Yes, ma'am," and, "No, ma'am." We had also put her in ballet when she was four, and that lasted until she was in her teens before she lost interest. The ballet helped for a while. She had become a little too much of a tomboy for her mother's liking, hanging around with her older brother and idolizing him the way she did.

I remember how when she was only two, we had taken her to church one Sunday in a new pair of black patent leather shoes. She loved those shoes from the moment we put them on her feet. She was amazed by the shiny leather. They had a hard bottom on them, and she was standing on the pew beside her mother. She found that if she stomped her feet on the wooden pew, the new shoes made a loud echoing sound. Our church back then was mostly wood—wooden floors, wooden walls, wooden pews—so the sound carried. At first, it was just one-foot stomp. She liked the sound, so she stomped both feet. My wife reached over and popped her on the legs and told her to stop. The little princess moved over a few feet out of my wife's reach and stomped again, looking to make sure that she was pissing her mother off as much as possible. She was only two and the battle for control between the two had already started. My wife slid just a little down the pew toward the kid and gave her a little smack on her bare legs to get her to stop. My daughter also got the mother look that said with her eyes, "I will kill you when we get home if you do that again." Again, my daughter moved just a few steps down the pew, and this time with more defiance than I thought a two-year-old capable of, she stomped her new shoes loud enough to make the whole congregation turn around and look. My wife quickly picked up the child and took her out of the church and into the vestibule between the front doors of the church and the main church. My wife began to spank her lacy little bottom for all she was worth.

When they returned to the church, I leaned over and whispered to my wife to look behind her at the wall between the vestibule and the church. She did and immediately noticed that the wall for the vestibule did not go all the way to the ceiling. The entire congregation was laughing at the young mother and her defiant little girl.

My wife tried hard to make my daughter a "girly girl," as she called them. Even after seven years of ballet, the child liked jazz better, and she and her brother actually became good competitive dancers during the '80s disco years. When our daughter was four years old, my wife entered her in the Miss Fourth of July contest at the Big Pier in Fairhope. She won second place, and Lisa Baugh won the top title. My wife swore that the only reason that the five-year-old Lisa had won was because she had curtsied and my four-year-old tomboy would not.

As my daughter grew up, she had a chance to become what she wanted. The balance between a tomboy and a lady worked out well in my opinion. I had taught both the kids to fish. My daughter loved to hunt white-tailed deer and scuba dive. The three of us hunted together for years. My daughter and I liked to hunt, but like me, her favorite place was the beach house. She spent hours on the end of this pier, reading hundreds of books while lying in the sun and getting as brown as a pecan shell.

One year when she was in her thirties, I got a frantic phone call from Trip, who was Obie's son-in-law. Trip and Obie's daughter Kathy still live next door. Trip was a little hard to understand when he called, but it was something about my daughter and her friends. He said something about a handgun and screaming coming from next door. My wife and I were in Fairhope, and it would take us an hour to get there. He wanted to know if I thought it was a good idea to go next door and have a look. It was about ten o'clock in the morning, and I could not imagine what was going on. "Go, Trip. Run. Hell, I don't know what's going on!" Trip dropped the phone without hanging up, and I could hear footsteps running across the floor. I could hear the gunshots. There must have been a dozen or more. Between every six shots, I heard sidesplitting laughter that obviously belonged to females.

I waited for what seemed like an hour but was probably only ten minutes, and then Trip returned to the phone. It seems that my daughter and two of her friends, who were all in their thirties, had gone down to the beach house the night before. They had been having a good time, and when they woke up at around eight o'clock, they had made a pitcher of Bloody Marys. One pitcher led to another, and slightly intoxicated, the three of them had decided to move the party to the pier.

On their way to the pier, they had almost stepped on a nine-inch-long baby water moccasin. Instead of thinking to get a shovel to kill the thing, the Calamity Jane I had raised got her handgun out of her car.

Understanding that alcohol was involved, I can make all kinds of excuses, but the Lady Smith & Wesson was empty and reloaded several times without the snake being in any mortal danger. Trip stood on the edge of the lot between our properties and watched the tipsy girls try to shoot the little snake. Once the gun was empty and before Calamity Jane could reload, Trip took the gun back to his house and got a simple garden rake to kill the scared little snake.

The girls were mad that Trip had spoiled their fun and told him so. He watched in disbelief as two of them headed for the pier in very small bathing suits while my lovely daughter headed for the house to mix more drinks. Trip finally came back to the phone to tell me what had happened. He actually got pissed off at me when I laughed at him for being so mad at the girls.

My daughter stands beside me now in her fifties. She and I have reversed roles in a lot of ways. Neither of us is comfortable with this turn of events. I have always taken care of everything from mowing her yard to helping her clean our boat. She has been married for a couple of years. Thank goodness after a string of loser boyfriends, she finally found the right guy. With her mother and me as role models for a lifelong marriage, I often wonder why she couldn't figure that partnership out before now.

Now that I can't take care of everything for her and her mother anymore, it has been hard on us all. I worry what will happen to the two ladies in my life now that I can't take care of them anymore. I only hope that I've taught them both enough over the years to be able to stand on their own two feet if I'm not here.

The beer and ice go into the cooler, and she sits down on the small table in between the two benches that make a ninety-degree angle at the corner of the pier. She has always sat on that end table instead of on the bench. I've noticed it a hundred times, but I've never asked her why.

"Daddy, I love you," she started, unable to hold back the tears.

"I'm not ready for this," she said. "We can't make it without you. We can't! Mom and I say we can, but nothing makes sense without you here. I have a hundred … no, a thousand things that I need to tell you every day."

She leans back and looks at the upper deck above her head. There is nothing there, but it keeps the tears in her eyes instead of running down her face.

"Like … I have this really crazy manager right now, and she is making me nuts. She says nice things to our employees, but you can tell from the look in her eyes that she doesn't mean a bit of it. Nobody trusts a thing she says." My daughter and I have had hundreds of discussions about human resources over the years. She has been in the HR business for more than thirty years, and I was in the business for thirty years before and during that same time.

"I think she may actually be evil," she continues. "So who am I going to talk to if you're not here to listen? Nobody knows HR stuff like you do."

My baby is crying. Why is she crying? I want to say, "Honey, I'm right here," but nothing comes out. Being a dad is the hardest thing I've ever done. There are times when my brain wants so bad to say just the right thing, but I'm scared to say the wrong thing. I wouldn't hurt this kid for any amount of money, and I worry that I will. There have been times when there was nothing else to do but just sit there and let her cry. This is one of those times.

"And I have this big project that I need to do before October. I have to present to a damn admiral in the navy. Who is going to help me with that presentation? *Who?*"

My daughter is the most independent thing in the world, and she still thinks she needs her dad like she did when she was six. When she was a kid, it was like watching her own mother grow up. She is as stubborn and opinionated. She also loves as deeply and cares about helping others just like her mom.

"Damn it," she pounds her clinched fist on the railing of the pier. "This is not fair. I can't do this."

She has no idea, but she can do whatever she needs to do. She inherited her mother's strong nature. I have been lucky and unlucky at the same time with these two independent women who think they have depended on me. There is righteousness and privilege in that kind of faith and love.

"Dad, do you remember when I was twenty-six and dating Kevin?" Kevin was the ex-husband that her mother and I hated. We hated him with every fiber of our being, but she loved him with every fiber of hers. Yes, unfortunately, I remembered him.

"I told you then that I didn't need your opinion. Remember? You said that Kevin was a big mistake, and I said that I was twenty-six and I needed to make my own decisions. I said I didn't need your opinion or approval." She cried and said, "Daddy, I was wrong. I need your opinions every day on everything."

This woman who had faced down CEOs is crying for her dad. My God, it is almost too much to bear.

"I love you, Dad. You are the most important mentor in my life. I just hope like hell that I have not disappointed you."

She gets up and starts back down the pier. From the back she looks even more like her mom the older she gets. She walks, looking down at her feet or through the boards of the pier. I can't tell from where I'm sitting. She sees the crab trap in the water, and out of habit, she pulls it up to check if anything has crawled in. There's a small crab in the net, too small to keep. She recognizes this immediately and throws the trap back in the water. I see a smile on her face, and she tosses the trap back in. I've done a good job with that kid.

This pier was built around crabbing with these traps. The southwest side of the pier does not have benches, so we can use this open space for the crab traps when they need to be out of the water. We will run about four crab traps a year. These are the wire traps, and after many years we have settled on the ones that are painted red as the best ones. I don't really know if the color of the trap is vital, but we find that for some unknown reason, the crabs in Mobile Bay are drawn more to the red ones than the ones that are not painted. We space the traps some six to eight feet apart, and on an average day, we will take in anywhere from twenty to forty crabs. Our crabs are called blue claw crabs. Over time we have set a harvest standard at forty crabs. Once the traps hold forty, it is time to take them out and cook them on the propane cooker in the backyard. I did not come up with the magic number of forty. My wife and daughter did. Forty is the number that they together can clean in one sitting without their fingers bleeding and hurting for days.

Every family has their traditions. One of ours is the cleaning of crabs every weekend. We put out the traps on Friday along with the ice for the beer, and we check the traps regularly all weekend. When we arrive, if there are more than forty crabs, my wife immediately has me empty the traps and cook the crabs. If there is less than that, I may get to wait until the next morning to cook them. My two girls have crab cleaning down to a science. My wife cleans the bodies, and my daughter cleans the claws. It has taken years of negotiation to reach this understanding; however, it works for them, and I stay the hell out of the way.

The wonder of this weekly event is that the two of them get to talk about everything. Anyone else who may sit down on the porch or the pier only gets to listen. They will review what has happened since the last time they sat together—who they have seen this week, what events are coming up next week, who is getting married or divorced, who has called, come by, sent an email, or posted on Facebook. And they go on for hours, sitting there together and cleaning crabs.

I have never timed how long it takes them to clean forty crabs, but it doesn't matter. It is a mother-daughter activity. They both look forward to this time together. They are both a little hyper, and they both believe that sitting still is a waste of time. The ritual of cleaning crabs gives them something to do with their hands while they engage their mouths and hearts. The two of them have spent hours over the years cleaning crabs. My wife has arthritis now and knows that cleaning these small treasures hurts her hands, but it doesn't stop her from this girl time together. I've watched her the day after cleaning crabs wince in pain when she picked up a coffee cup, but I don't think she would give up the time if they threatened to cut off her fingers. They love the time together, and I love to watch and listen.

I have learned over the years to stay out of the middle of these two strong women. I've seen my fourteen-year-old daughter scream at my wife and say that she hated her. I've also heard my wife scream that she was going to kill her only daughter the very minute she walked through the door when she was late coming home. I have stood back and seen both of them fight and fuss like their lives depended on winning a battle, but I have also seen them turn on their very best friends when the friends had said something negative about the other.

One of my wife's very best friends made the mistake of agreeing with my wife when she was railing about my daughter's latest boyfriend. She was just agreeing with my wife and said something like "Isn't she smarter than going out with that loser?" We all thought it. We all said it to one another. Hell, my wife had said it herself a thousand times. But God help her friend when she made a derogatory comment about my wife's baby girl. I don't think they actually spoke again for a couple of weeks. Her friend was confused. She had not said anything that everybody else wasn't saying, including my wife. She had made one mistake. She said it out loud to her mother.

The same was true of my daughter. She claimed many times in her teens to hate her mother. They both screamed and yelled. She slammed doors and rolled her eyes at her mother. She slammed down phones and mumbled things under her breathe about her mom. She would go out with guys just one more time because she knew that her mother didn't approve. But by God, they were just alike. More than one young man told me very confidentially that "she is just like her mother." They both denied they were anything alike. My daughter would become quite indignant that she was nothing like her mother. Then she would turn and storm off just as I had seen her mother do a million times. But God help us all if you said something negative to one about the other.

I remember taking the phone out of my daughter's hand more than once when my wife was an elected official in the Baldwin County Court system. My daughter was a believer in truth and justice but not necessarily freedom of speech when it came to her mother. She always wanted to call the local newspaper and "tell them the true story" when they were critical of anything happening in the circuit clerk's office, which my wife ran. We had a saying in our house. "You can't fight people who buy ink by the barrel." I think that is truer in the digital social media age than ever before. My daughter never thought this was true. She has always wanted to fight the press when it came to her mother. My wife was an amazingly popular politician. She worked hard and remembered where we came from. She was loved by many people, even though they were required by the state of Alabama to write her checks for everything from child support to alimony to speeding tickets, which no one ever wants to write. With political office comes adversity. My daughter couldn't get beyond it. She hated my wife's job because politics was the meanest game in any town. But my daughter was my wife's second biggest supporter behind me because she was immensely proud of her and the things she was doing for the state of Alabama. They were a pair. The only hope I held was that they did not turn on me at the same time. If I had one of them on my side, I had a fifty-fifty shot of making it to live another day.

I remember one anniversary when I had been working long hours and traveling a lot. Things were very busy at the printing company at that point. Who knows what the issues were at that time, but it was always something when you manage that much money and that many people. I had come home late, and my daughter was waiting on me. It was the day before my anniversary, and she was sitting up, obviously in vigil for me. She demanded to know what I had gotten her mother for our anniversary. I had told her truthfully that I had gotten her mother a rose for our anniversary.

"A rose?" she had questioned.

"Yes, a single red rose," I told her. I was making fairly decent money at that point. Our house was paid for, and we were finished with the beach house. The kid was horrified that I was a cheap bastard and that all I had gotten my wife for our anniversary was a single cheap rose.

She was pissed off and tried over the next twenty-four hours to convince me that the stores were still open and that if I needed her to go shopping with me, she would. I held tight. No, the rose I had gotten was the perfect anniversary gift, and I thought that no other presents were needed.

My daughter was horrified. I was a shithead to this teenager.

My wife and I were headed to dinner that night. I had made reservations at the Grand Hotel in Point Clear. I had a great night planned to thank this woman whom I could not have lived a minute without. But before all that, I had a little girl to teach a lesson. I had asked my wife to open her present in front of my daughter. She agreed with a wink from me. She did not know what was up, but she knew who it was directed to.

My wife opened her gift, my daughter rolling her eyes and waiting for the polite response from my wife. My wife opened her gift and began to cry. Assuming that I had messed up again, my daughter did not understand when my wife jumped up and hugged me with all her might. My daughter got up and crossed the room to look in the box that my wife had just opened. Enclosed in white delicate paper in the box was a Beame Porcelain Rose, a collector's piece that my wife had lusted after for months at the local jewelry store. She could have afforded to buy it herself, but she had not been comfortable spending the money on herself. She was delighted, and to this day, she cherishes the piece. A single rose has always been our thing as a couple. It is a private sign for us of our love, the one true love, the one best friend, the one who knew you and your secrets, the only one you can count on.

It was additionally nice because my kid had to eat crow that night, which is an acquired taste for all teenagers.

Yes, my girls are something else. They are so much alike yet so different. My daughter had a lot of me in her. She followed my lead into the outdoors. She is a hunter and fisherman. The only outdoor sport she ever did that I did not approve of was scuba diving. It scared me. I had lost a good friend in a diving accident, and I fought my daughter doing the sport. But she loved it, and her instructors told me that she was good at it. I had spent a great deal of money to make sure that she had the very best gear when she started, but it made me nervous every time she left the dock. I waited for that call to come back, saying that they were back to the dock safely for the first couple of years. She knew how I felt and made a point, even when she was older than forty, to call her dad the minute she got off the boat from a dive trip.

My girls were special. They were the focus on my life. But it was my son that broke my heart clean in two. I guess we need to discuss that.

CHAPTER 16

We have made it this far down memory lane, it is just a little bit further down the road to go, but we need to stop here and deal with a pothole. It is more like a complete washout of the lane than a pothole. If I am going to be truthful about my life, I need to get this part over with now.

As I've told you, my son, Danny, loved this beach house. Danny had lived here for a while when he and my wife started their own business. He had spent endless hours on this pier, fishing with his friends or just hanging out. During his junior year in high school, he and his buddies started the annual Fort Morgan Road Six-Pack Crew Fishing Tournament. It was a long name for a competition that had more to do with boys being boys than fishing. The first year the winning fish was a six-inch-long perch. There was a great deal of alcohol consumed, but the pictures of the fish told the truth.

My son and my wife had opened their business after he had spent two years at the University of Alabama and decided that college was not his thing. He had come home and moved to the beach, which may be every young man's dream.

Their business had taken off after the first year of the linen service, and the second year they were able to work sixty hours a week instead of a hundred like they did the first year. The season, which ran from Memorial Day to Labor Day, was grueling. These fourteen weeks a year at the beach were when you either made your money for the year or didn't. If you didn't make enough money during the summer, it was hard to keep yourself going through the winter at that time. You had to make enough money to carry you through the winter. Everything at the beach revolved around the summer calendar. We took vacations during the winter when everyone else was taking them during the summer. My son scheduled his wedding in February during the off-season. Those weeks ruled our lives for the time that we had that business. Now Gulf Shores is totally different. In the early 1990s, a group of Northerners we call snowbirds—because they fly south for the winter from Michigan and other cold places—discovered Gulf Shores and moved in for the winter months. The money still isn't as good during the winter as it is during the summer, but it helps keep some of the businesses open.

Danny had been dating a lovely girl named Perian for several years during high school and college, and in February 1982, he decided to settle down and get married. They had a beautiful big wedding. They moved away from the beach and into a little house on Fish River. She worked in Mobile, and he worked at the beach, so their house was in the middle. Danny bought a motorcycle because it was cheap transportation. He wasn't new to motorcycles. Both the kids had ridden them for years. Six weeks after they got married, Danny had gone to a friend's house to play pool and had never come home. He was found the next morning by a local farmer who was driving down the road and saw his motorcycle off to the side of the road in a ditch.

The night before had been foggy, and he had driven straight through an S-curve in the road to his house. He was only a hundred yards from his driveway when it happened. It is impossible to know what really happened, but it appeared that another car had been coming in the opposite direction. The combination of the fog and the lights must have caused him to lay the motorcycle over into a skid. The motorcycle had hit the ditch and flipped over several times, landing on my son at least once, maybe more. The result was a broken neck and most everything else broken too.

I was at the Florida plant working when the call came in that I needed to get back to Alabama as quickly as possible. My boss, generally a major ass, had sent a corporate jet to pick me up in Lakeland, Florida, and drop me on a dirt airstrip in Gulf Shores, Alabama. I didn't know what the problem was until I reached the small private airport in Gulf Shores. I was told that my son was in an accident, but nobody had the heart to tell me he was dead at twenty-one years old. I was met by several cars of friends and a police escort at the airport, and we drove the few miles to the linen service. My wife had been sitting in her office with a police officer who had come to tell her earlier that morning that her son had been found and that he was dead. The linen service provided the bed linens for the Gulf Shores Police Department, so most of the cops knew my wife and my son, who delivered to them daily. Jackie had asked the officer to stay with her until somebody else arrived, and being the small town that Gulf Shores was then and it being the off-season, he had agreed. She sat there silently with the police office, making a list of pallbearers for her oldest child, her only son, and her business partner. She is a remarkably strong woman and had held it together, opening the business and giving out job assignments to the staff for the day. He even handled a distraught daughter when she arrived from work just forty-five minutes before my flight landed.

It was April 1, 1982, and our lives had all changed forever. My wife possesses a tremendous amount of strength, and her logic took over in this situation. She was in full-blown planning mode when I got out of the car that had picked me up. I don't remember walking across the Shell parking lot to the linen service. I remember my wife's arms around me and her holding me to keep me from crumpling into a heap on the ground. While she reacted with superhuman strength, I reacted from the heart and the gut. My mind stopped working that day. I'm not really sure what you call it, but day and night, I walked around in a fog. I lost time that I'll never get back. There were days and weeks that I don't remember. I don't remember getting up, going to work, coming home, or going to sleep. My family would catch me standing somewhere and looking at nothing. People told me that I had a blank, lost look on my face for months.

I was instructed to take several weeks off my regular job, which we needed because not only had we lost our son but we had lost the co-owner of a family business. We needed time to regroup. The effect on my wife was that she worked harder. My daughter came to work for us after she got off work from her regular job at night and every weekend. I worked harder physically than I had worked in years, but I was not mentally present at all. The physical part of the job was a safe place for me. It was the physical work that kept my body moving, which minimized my thinking. I did okay holding it together if I was working; however, when the day was done and there was nothing to focus on, my mind grew into itself, and my thoughts carried me to a very dark and lonely place.

I would get off work in the evenings, exhausted, and walk to the end of this pier. I'd sit here, and the deep recesses of my soul would scream about how unfair it all had been. I had worked hard. I didn't deserve this. I was a good father. I loved my family. It should have been me, not Danny. It should have been somebody else's kid, not mine. Every dark and dangerous thought you can imagine went through my mind. I ignored my wife and daughter. I didn't really give a shit what they were going through. I was so deep into my own hell that I saw no way out.

After several weeks of working for my wife, my boss at the printing company called to find out when I would return. All the sudden, my job, my career, and my life made no sense at all to me. The corporate games, the personnel problems, all the issues with vendors and equipment, none of it made any difference to me, and I saw it as a total waste of energy. I instantly hated the job and career that I had worked so hard to build. It had made me miss so much of my kids' lives, so many important events. It was so consuming that even when I was with my kids and wife, I was thinking about work and what I needed to do the next day … or week … or month.

I tried to go back to work. I tried to be interested in the career that I had worked to build for so many years. For a couple of weeks, I thought I did a pretty good job of faking it, but I could not focus. Something happened to the wiring in my brain, and everything was short-circuiting. In late June, I walked into my boss's office and put down the keys to my office, the company car, my company credit cards, and my employee badge on his desk. Boyd, my boss of almost fifteen years, looked up at me and asked what was going on. I told him that I could not do it anymore. He asked if I needed more time off or if I needed a change of assignment. Maybe I could stay local instead of traveling so much for a while. He said a lot of things that made sense, but I was too confused to listen. I left his office and had to bum a ride home because I had been driving a company car for years. I guess I should have thought about giving up the company car before I walked out.

It was not just the death of my son, but I'm sure that was the straw that broke the camel's back. It was everything. Being involved in corporate life had taken me away from my kids and my wife. It had turned me into somebody I didn't know and didn't like. I was drinking too much with clients and spending time with customers instead of my family. Now my son was gone, and all of a sudden, the plan to make it up to them later was over. There was no later to give them. My father had missed my childhood, and I always wanted to be the better father. I had done a good job with the kids. I knew that, but I had missed so much. I really wondered how much better I had done than my father. Sure, I had given them all the things that money could buy, which my father hadn't done. I had been there in the early years when they were in Little League and ballet. But now it was all over. I was forty-one, and I felt like I was done.

If this happened today, they would just give me a pill—Prozac or something like it—to make me happy. But in the early '80s, we still dealt with our issues the good old-fashioned way, namely with alcohol-induced breakdowns. Once I found a ride home, I came out on the end of this pier, and I sat. I spent days doing nothing but thinking and drinking. There were nights that I slept on the end of this pier. My wife would come out and throw a blanket over me, but I didn't know that until I woke up in the morning.

A couple of days into sitting on the end of this pier, I looked down the beach and saw something that had washed up overnight. I walked down the beach and found an old stump in the shallow water. I pulled the stump onto the sand and had a good look at it. Then I carried the heavy stump back to the pier. It must have weighted fifty pounds, and it was wet and sandy. I sat with that stump on the end of this pier, and we had a little talk. We talked for days, me and my stump. We drank beer together. I yelled and cussed at the stump. I told the stump secrets that I could not even tell my best friend, Mark. The stump and I cried a great deal, working through the stages of grief, though I didn't know it at the time. At the time, I thought that damn piece of a tree was my only confidant in the world.

Just like today, friends and family came to the end of the pier. They talked to me and tried to tell me everything I already knew. I needed to move on. Danny was in a better place. Life moves on. And the biggest lie—time heals all wounds. They said I still had a wonderful wife and daughter who needed me. None of this mattered. I didn't care. My stump was my friend and the only thing that understood me. Everyone, including my wife and daughter, thought I was stark raving mad. And maybe I was. After all, I was talking to a stump.

This went on for more than a week. I wasn't going to work. I wasn't eating. All I did was talk to my stump and drink. My wife's strength and understanding were the only thing that saved me from my madness. She eventually had enough. She walked out to the end of the pier after a long day of working her ass off in the hot linen service, doing the job of two people herself, and she sat down beside me. We sat for a minute in silence. She looked at me, and I looked at my stump. We both understood that I had lost it. There was no question about that. And then in her own special way, she explained that it was enough. She told me to get my ass up and go take a shower. Dinner would be on the table in the kitchen in thirty minutes, and she said, "Your clean feet had better be under that table." She stood up and started walking down the pier. She called back over her shoulder, "And throw that damn piece of wood in the swamp!"

I did as directed, and as everyone had promised, life did go on eventually. It was not the same life, but after a long time, it was a good life just the same. I still miss my son, and I wonder what he would have been like in his thirties and forties. My daughter was a very different person at each of those ages, and I would have enjoyed him more now than ever.

My time on the end of this pier with the stump always reminded me of Wilson, the volleyball in the movie *Castaway*. Tom Hanks befriended the ball when he was alone on an island. My stump was my Wilson, and this pier was my island. Thank God for Jackie Calhoun and the lifeline that she threw me to pull me back.

I was angry with God for many years after that. I wouldn't attend a wedding or a funeral for more than twenty years. I would not walk into a church for any function regardless of whom or what was involved. I don't know why I thought it mattered that I didn't go to church. I was hurting people I loved, not getting even with God. He always wins after all.

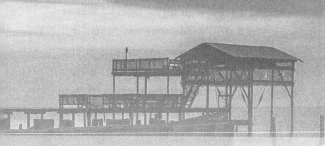

Chapter 17

Now there is a sight! I look down the pier and a lovely young girl of fourteen years old is walking straight toward me with two other girls who are twelve and ten. Along with my wife and daughter, these three are my favorite girls in the world. We can also add their mother into that group.

When my daughter was forty, she decided that she wanted to be a foster parent. She was lucky enough to get a fifteen-year-old girl named Jessica. Jess had not had an easy time of it. Her parents were always in trouble, and she had gotten pregnant. When Jessica came to live with Donna, she had a six-week-old baby named Grace. We always called her Gracie, and she was the center of our universe. Jessica was a bright girl, and she got her life together and moved out of foster care at eighteen to live on her own. She had Gracie's two little sisters named Fallon and Korra later, and the three of them became known to all our friends as our grander-children.

The kids have all grown up so much now. It's hard to believe this teenager was once the cute little six-month-old that Jessica and Donna dressed up as a ladybug her first Halloween. Gracie has big bright eyes, and she was the best little ladybug ever. I taught all these girls to ride bikes, and I taught the younger two to swim at the Elks Lodge pool. When they were still little, we played the treasure hunter game with them. They were amazed that Mr. Doug had pirates as relatives and that they had buried treasure on our beach.

Of all the blessings we have had in our lives, these three are some of the biggest.

"Ow, damn it," Korra said as she stumped her toe on one of the boards on the deck of the pier that stuck up a little too high.

"Don't use that language, Korra," Fallon says.

"Good grief, Fallon! It was only damn! It's not like she said something really bad," Gracie argues. "And where the hell are your shoes, Korra?"

Korra is the tomboy of the three. She hates wearing shoes, and she would never wear a dress at this age unless it was something big. She has on a little dark blue dress but no shoes.

"You shouldn't be running around without your shoes, Korra. There are stickers in the yard," Fallon says.

"No, there is not. Pop cleaned all the stickers out, so I didn't have to wear shoes," Korra says.

"How do you know that?" Gracie says.

"Because he told me," Korra says and smiles.

These three kids had started out rough. Their mom didn't have much, and the two different dads didn't have much more. Their mom never married either of their dads, but that's her story and not mine.

My wife and I had been like grandparents to these kids when they were little, and even now we would spend as much time as we are allowed to with them. We would take them to the park down by the bay in Fairhope and walk as they fed the fish in the pond. We had to make sure that they didn't get too close and fall in. I made sure that all three of them knew how to ride bikes, and we bought their first bikes for them. When they were small and learning their colors, we would sit in the middle of the floor for hours and play with blocks. I read to all three of them when they were small, but Gracie was always the one who would get a book and climb up in my lap to have me read to her. They are way too big for that now. I miss those days when Pop could fix anything and he was the smartest guy around.

They love to come over to Pop and Keke's house. That was what they called me and Jackie. It was a big place, and they had their own room with tons of dolls and stuffed toys. We bought a kitchen set and all three of them had played with it for years before they outgrew it.

Korra was always amazed by the computer, and she would sit in my lap for hours and play computer games on my lap. She wasn't big enough to sit in the chair alone back then and reach the controls by herself.

"Remember when Pop used to take us to the store in the truck?" Fallon says.

"Yeah, he would let you have all the change out of his ashtray," Korra adds.

"You could buy whatever you wanted," Gracie says and laughs. "And if you really wanted something and didn't have enough change, he would always make up the difference."

"Pop was always at my ballet classes. Even when my own dad couldn't make it," Fallon adds.

"You know that we are not even related to them—Pop and Keke— right?" Gracie says.

"But they never looked at us like that. They treat us just like we are their grandchildren," Fallon says.

All three girls sit quietly and don't say anything. What they don't realize is that they mean more to us than anything. They have given my wife and me more joy and more memories than any real grandchildren could have.

One of our favorite things to do every year was have the Pop and Keke Christmas for the kids. We would invite the girls and a few of their cousins to a Christmas party. They would get presents, and we would have what Fallon called a "pretty dinner." Jackie would break out all the crystal and silver, and we would serve hot dogs, fried chicken, and chips on silver trays. They went through a phase where they liked strawberries and chocolate served on silver trays. My wife had tons of that stuff, and as we grew older, we didn't entertain much at the house in Fairhope, so we didn't use all her expensive dinnerware and crystal glasses. So once a year these kids had their pretty dinner.

There are very few people more important to me than these three young ladies.

CHAPTER 18

It has taken me a long time to say everything that I needed to say. The group of people in the front yard of the beach house has grown. Everybody seems to be here, but strangely enough, they seem overdressed. I need to wander up there and find out what is going on. But I want just a few more minutes of this solitude. It's so comfortable sitting here on the pier and watching from a distance.

I hear something behind me and turn to see a small aluminum boat coming this way. People are always coming over by boat, so this isn't unusual. I wonder who it is.

Mark and Barbara Dee would come over by boat when they lived on Fish River. That was always fun. Especially when the traffic was busy during the season, they could just scoot right across the bay and be here in about thirty minutes.

As the boat gets closer, I notice that there is only one person in the boat—a young man with his back to me, watching over his shoulder at the wake behind the boat. I can tell that he has blond hair and a good tan. He is wearing white shorts, and strangely enough, he has on a linen service blue T-shirt. That's strange because I haven't seen any of those shirts for twenty years or more. Jackie had a pile of them for several years, but I thought she finally got rid of all of them. Somebody must still have one or two.

The dark hunter-green aluminum boat is about thirty yards from the end of the pier when the driver of the boat turns around to sit toward the front, and I see his face for the first time.

No, this can't be right. The small boat pulls up to the dock, and the young man throws a line over the post and quickly ties it up.

"Hey, Dad," the young man says.

"Danny?" I ask.

"Yep. Surprise!" he says and laughs, giving me that notorious smile that I remember from more than thirty years ago. How could I forget that smile? I paid for braces to make sure those teeth were straight.

"I don't understand," I say, shaking my head to clear this illusion.

"Sure you do." Danny steps off the boat and onto the pier. My son walks up the steps and on to the main deck of the pier where I stand stupefied.

Danny walks over to Dad's ice chest and gets out a Miller Lite. Then he looks up the pier to the crowd gathering on the grass.

"Big crowd. You really had a positive effect on a lot of people's lives, Dad," says my son, who has been dead for more than thirty years. "That's more than most people can say."

He wipes the ice off the bottom of the can and takes a drink of his beer. He closes his eyes and faces toward the warm sun. It's like he hasn't changed one bit. He is as young and alive as never before.

"But … you're dead?" I say with a flair for the obvious.

"Yes, I am," he says sadly. "And now so are you."

Danny turns his back on me and walks to the railing at the front of the pier. He puts one foot up on the bench and both hands on the railing. After looking for a few minutes, studying the people in the front yard, he says, "This is the hard part, Dad. The letting go is the hardest part. It's hard knowing that those people up there still love you and need you."

I know that what he is saying is true. I don't want to leave them. They need me. I need them. Even though my wife and I have planned for this day for years, I'm not ready to go. And then my son turns around to smile at me again. All the worry and pain is gone. All the plans and problems don't seem to matter anymore. I realize that I feel better, more alive than I have in ages. I look down, and I'm standing up straight and tall, not that old-man stooped over walk that my Jackie was always telling me about. When she would see my shoulder stooped from getting old, she'd say, "Byron, stand up straight. You look like an old man!" There is no pain in my chest or my stomach. I take a step forward, and it's easy. There's no swelling in my feet!

I look at my son and realize that this is what pain-free feels like.

"Granddad Eric came to get me. Merle came to get Eric, of course. I came to get you," he explains and smiles. "It makes it easier if they send somebody you know."

"We had a whole group of people who wanted to come get you," he adds. "But I won. Eric and Merle both wanted to come. Merle was pretty firm about her opinion. Granny Emily, your mom, wanted to come, but she backed down to Merle. Obie pissed everybody off because he said it was him who you really wanted to see first. Aunt Suzanne just sat back and let everybody else argue over it, but she has always hated confrontation with that crowd."

"You won?" I ask.

"Yeah, in the end, we settled it by playing cards for it, and I won." Danny smiles.

"Cards?" I'm stunned. "You played cards to see who would come get me to take me to where? Heaven?"

"You got it!" He laughs. He's more handsome than I remember. He's still tall and looks like he's twenty-two. His eyes are bright and clear. His smile is white and seems warm. By God, this is Danny. My Danny. My son is right here. I walk the few steps over to him and hug him with all the strength I have. And by God, he hugs me back! After a minute, he pushes away and looks at me square in the eye.

Again, he turns away and looks at the people in the yard. "Mom looks more beautiful every year," he says. "And my pain-in-the-ass sister looks like she turned out okay."

He looks over his shoulder at me and then adds, "She is going to take it the hardest, you know. You being gone. Little sis plays like she is tough, but she is a wimp really! But you must know that they will be okay in time. They tell you all kinds of stuff, but that part is true."

Danny stands for a moment, more looking at the group that was gathering around my wife and his mother. "They'll all take care of her.

"Look, I know that you have about a thousand questions. I get that. We all do when we get picked up. But we have a bit of a trip, and I'll have time to answer most of them," he says.

He turns and looks at me. "Well, we need to go." He smiles and walks toward the boat that's still tied to the dock.

"We are on a schedule," he says and laughs. "Mom used to say that all the time. I hated when she said that!"

"Can I ask one question?" I ask, moving toward him and the boat.

"Sure. Ask all the questions you need," he says.

"What kind of card game did you win?" I smile and put my arm around his shoulder. He's real. He's solid, not a ghost.

"You kidding me? Go Fish. It was Merle's decision what to play!" he says and laughs.

Printed in the United States
By Bookmasters